For Catherine Rock with pleasure, and with admiration for your work
Carter Revard
Ludlow, 29 July 2010

How the Songs Come Down

CARTER REVARD, Osage on his father's side, grew up on the Osage Reservation in Oklahoma. After work as farm hand and greyhound trainer, he took B.A.s from the University of Tulsa and Oxford (Rhodes Scholarship, Oklahoma and Merton 1952), was given his Osage name and a Yale Ph.D., then taught medieval and American Indian literatures before retiring in 1997. He has published *Ponca War Dancers; Cowboys and Indians, Christmas Shopping; An Eagle Nation; Family Matters, Tribal Affairs;* and *Winning the Dust Bowl*, as well as translations into heroic couplets of X-rated fabliaux (published in *The Chaucer Review*). He has also won fame in the Footnote Stakes by piling high and deep proof that the scribe of the Harley Lyrics, who copied those fabliaux, was a Ludlow Lad ("O down in lovely muck he's lain"), very like Absalom in *The Miller's Tale*, who died *in medias res* (1349) of the Black Death. (One Harley Lyricist describes standing at a window and kissing the girl, but unlike Absalom this lad kissed the right orifice, and was invited in.)

Earthworks Series
Series Editor: Janet McAdams

How the Songs Come Down

NEW AND SELECTED POEMS

CARTER REVARD

SALT

CAMBRIDGE

PUBLISHED BY SALT PUBLISHING
PO Box 937, Great Wilbraham, Cambridge PDO CB1 5JX United Kingdom

© Carter Revard, 2005

The right of Carter Revard to be identified as the
author of this work has been asserted by him in accordance
with Section 77 of the Copyright, Designs and Patents Act 1988.

First published 2005

Printed and bound in the United Kingdom by Lightning Source

Typeset in Swift 9.5 / 13

ISBN 1 84471 064 5 paperback

SP

1 3 5 7 9 8 6 4 2

Dedication
to

the small birds only
whose life continues on the gourd,
whose life continues in our dance,
that flutter as the gourd is rattled and
we dance to honor on a sunbright day
and in the moonbright night
the little girl being brought in,
becoming one of us,
as once was done for me,
for each of us who dance.
The small birds only, who have given
their bodies that a small girl
may live to see old age.
I have called them here
to set them into song
who made their rainbow bodies long before
we came to earth,
who learning song and flight became
beings for whom the inflnite sky
and trackless ocean are
a path to spring:
now they will sing and we
are dancing with them, here.

Contents

Acknowledgments

Some of these poems were published in Ponca War Dancers and Cowboys and Indians, Christmas Shopping: I am grateful to Frank Parman and Arn Henderson of Point Riders Press. Others appeared in An Eagle Nation, Winning the Dust Bowl, and Family Matters, Tribal Affairs; I thank the University of Arizona Press and the editors of its Sun Tracks Series for permission to reprint those here. Some have appeared over the years in the following journals, to whose editors I give thanks: the Massachusetts Review, Iowa Review, Nimrod, The American Oxonian, Studies in American Indian Literature, American Indian Culture and Research Quarterly, Florilegium. Other poems in this collection have not previously been published.

I am very grateful for residencies that helped write and revise: in 1994 at the Millay Colony for the Arts; in 1996 at the Villa Serbelloni in Bellagio, Italy; in 1998 at the MacDowell Colony; in 2002 in Mojàcar, Spain, with the Fundación Valparaíso. In autumn 1997, I had spousal housal at the Villa dei Pini of the Bogliasco Foundation, while my wife wrote on Pindar and Milton and swam on sunny days in the Golfo di Paradiso. My sisters Maxine, Ireta, and Josephine; my brothers Antwine, Jim, and Junior; my Aunt Jewell and all her children have given invaluable time in Buck Creek and White Eagle, on remembered roads and streams and meadows, in many worlds. Kathryn and Charles Red Corn more recently, and over many years Grandma Josephine, Uncle Kenneth, Aunt Arita, Flora and family, and Aunt Jewell, have been there for and with me at the Pawhuska and White Eagle dances. Evelyne Wahkinney Voelker and family taught some of the ways of Gourd Dancers. Frank and Sarah in Norman, Norma and Jerry in South Dakota, are friends I treasure. Janet McAdams made this book possible: to her, Chris, and Jen I am truly grateful.

To my Osage, Ponca, Scotch-Irish and Irish and French brothers and sisters, parents and grandparents, uncles and aunts, cousins and kinfolk and friends, I owe my being and what I can manage to give back with thanks. When I dedicate this book to the small birds, it is also for all my relations, through time and space. I have been very lucky to have them to learn from, as also from teachers in schools from whom to learn: Mrs. Fisher, Mrs. Ridgeway, Miss Conner, Mr. Loyd; Miss Wentz, Miss Spencer, Señorita Newkirk, Miss Paxton, Miss Corbin, Mr. Haley, Mr. Den Adel among others. And at the University of Tulsa, two wonderful teachers (among many fine ones), Eikenberry and Hayden; at Merton College, Oxford, Hugo Dyson and Geoffrey Smithers, and later Alan Robson and Roger Highfield and Norman Davis, showed me scholarly ways; at Yale, Louis Martz and Talbot Donaldson. At Amherst College my students did their best to educate me, Rolfe Humphries showed me ways to write, and I respect Ben DeMott as the most gifted and brilliant colleague I have known. I have admired and tried to learn some ways with words from Simon Ortiz, Wendy Rose, Robert Frost, Louise Erdrich, Scott Momaday, X. J. Kennedy. I have had good colleagues and friends at Washington University, St. Louis, and I have found libraries and librarians to be the best part of the civilized world, from the time Miss Conner (when I was in the sixth grade at Buck Creek) first brought that carload of books and stacked them onto the newly built bookshelves.

In some of these poems there are even references to our children and their beautiful mother, who has put up with me for almost fifty years. I hope they won't mind.

Indian Territory

Coyote Tells Why He Sings

There was a little rill of water, near the den,
That showed a trickle, all the dry summer
When I was born. One night in late August, it rained —
The Thunder waked us. Drops came crashing down
In dust, on stiff blackjack leaves, on lichened rocks,
And the rain came in a pelting rush down over the hill,
Wind blew wet into our cave as I heard the sounds
Of leaf-drip, rustling of soggy branches in gusts of wind.

And then the rill's tune changed—I heard a rock drop
That set new ripples gurgling, in a lower key.
Where the new ripples were, I drank, next morning,
Fresh muddy water that set my teeth on edge.
I thought how delicate that rock's poise was and how
The storm made music, when it changed my world.

Geode

I still remember ocean, how
she came in with all I wanted, how we opened
the hard shell we had made
of what she gave me and painted into
that lodge's white walls the shifting
rainbows of wave-spray—
I remember even the vague drifting
before the shell was made, my slow swimming
amidst the manna until I sank
down into stone, married, rooted there, joined
its stillness where the moving waters
would serve us as the moon would bring them by.
Growing, I remember how softness
of pale flesh secreted the smooth hardness
of shell, how the gritty pain
was healed with rainbow tears
of pearl,
I remember dreaming
of the new creatures flying through air
as the sharks swam through ocean
hallucinating feathers and dinosaurs,
pterodactyls and archæopteryxes,
great turquoise dragonflies
hovering, shimmering, hawking after the huge
mosquitoes fat with brontosaurus blood. And when
I died and the softness vanished inside
my shell and the sea flowed in I watched
it drying as the waters ebbed, saw how my bony whiteness held
at its heart the salty gel whose desire swelled
and grew and globed against the limey mud,
chalcedony selving edged and spiked its way
through dreams of being flowers trembling
against the wind, snowflakes falling
into a desert spring. But the rain
of limestone hardened round us and my walls

grew full of holes, I waked into
a continent of caves, a karst-land where
sweet water chuckled and trickled, siliceated through
my crevices as once the salty ocean had, and I felt
purple quartz-crystals blossom where
my pale flesh had been.
Then I knew my dream
was true, and I waited for
the soft hands to come down like a dream
and lift me into sunlight, give me there to diamond
saws that sliced me in two, to diamond dust that polished
my new selves of banded agate,
I let them separate and shelve them heavy
on either side of a word-hoard whose light leaves
held heavy thoughts between
the heavier, wiser, older lines of all
my mirrored selves, the wave-marks left
by snowflake-feathery amethyst
ways of being,
by all those words,
by the Word, made slowly,
slowly, in-
to Stone.

Stone Age

Whoever broke a rock first wasn't trying
to look inside it, surely—
was looking for an edge
or trying just to hammer with it, and it broke—
then he saw it glitter,
how BRIGHT inside it was; noticed how things
unseen are fresh. Maybe he said
it's like the sky, that when the sun has
crashed down through the west
breaks open to the Milky Way and we see
farther than we are seen for once, as far
as light and time can reach and almost over
the edge of time, its spiral track like agate
swirls in rock from when it still
was water-stains, had not yet found its
non-solution to the puzzle
of dissolution, keeping within its darkness
the traces of its origin as day keeps night and
night keeps stars.
Pebbles, headstones,
Altamira,
dust-wrinkles over darkness.
What shines within?

Skins as Old Testament

Wonder who first slid in
to use another creature's skin
for staying warm—blood-smeared
heresy almost, Hunter becoming
Deer, Shepherd the Lamb as in flamelit
Dordogne caves or dim cathedrals—
crawling inside the deer's
still-vivid presence there
to take their lives from what had moved
within, to eat delicious life
then spread its likeness over a sleeping
and breathing self, musk-wrapped
inside the wind,
the rain,
the sleet—
to roll up in a seal-skin self beneath
a mammoth heaven
on which the sleet would rap and tap,
to feel both feet
grow warm even on ice
or in the snow—hand-chalicing
new tallow flame as spirit
of passing life
and every time a tingling
revelation when the life
came back into a freezing hand or foot
after the fur embraced its flesh, still deeper
when human bodies coupling in
a bear's dark fur
found winter's warmth and then
its child
within the woman
came alive.

Dancing with Dinosaurs

Before we came to earth,
before the birds had come,
they were dinosaurs, their feathers
were a bright idea
that came this way:
see, two tiny creatures weighing
two ounces each keep quiet and among
the ferns observe bright-eyed
the monsters tear each other
and disappear; these two watch from
the edge of what, some fifty billion spins
of the cooling earth ahead, will be
called Nova Scotia—now, with reptilian
whistles they look southward as
Pan-Gaea breaks apart and lets
a young Atlantic send its thunder crashing
up to the pines where they cling
with minuscule bodies in a tossing wind,
September night in the chilly rain and
they sing, they spread
small wings to flutter out above
surf-spray and rise to
twenty thousand feet on swirling
winds of a passing cold front that lift
them over the grin of sharks southeastward into sun
and all day winging under him pass high above
the pink and snowy beaches of Bermuda flying
through zero cold and brilliance into darkness
then into moonlight over steel
Leviathans with their mimic pines that call them down
to rest and die—
they bear
southeast steadily but the Trade
Winds come and float them curving
back southward over the Windward Islands and

southwestward into marine and scarlet of
their third day coming down
to four thousand feet still winging over
Tobago, descending till
the scaled waves stretch and widen into the surf of
Venezuela and they drop
through moonlight down to perch
on South America's shoulder, having become
the Male and Female Singers, having
put on their feathers and survived.

2.

When I was named
a Thunder person, I was told:
here is a being
of whom you may make your body
that you may live to see old age: now
as we face the drum
and dance shaking the gourds, this gourd
is like a rainbow of feathers, lightly
fastened with buckskin,
fluttering as the gourd is shaken.
The eagle feathers I
have still not earned, it is
the small birds only
whose life continues on the gourd,
whose life continues in our dance,
that flutter as the gourd is rattled and
we dance to honor on a sunbright day
and in the moonbright night
the little girl being brought in,
becoming one of us,
as once was done for me,
for each of us who dance.

The small birds only, who have given
their bodies that a small girl
may live to see old age.
I have called them here
to set them into song
who made their rainbow bodies long before
we came to earth,
who learning song and flight became
beings for whom the infinite sky
and trackless ocean are
a path to spring:
now they will sing and we
are dancing with them, here.

Driving in Oklahoma

On humming rubber along this white concrete,
lighthearted between the gravities
of source and destination like a man
halfway to the moon
in this bubble of tuneless whistling
at seventy miles an hour from the windvents,
over prairie swells rising
and falling, over the quick offramp
that drops to its underpass and the truck
thundering beneath as I cross
with the country music twanging out my windows,
I'm grooving down this highway feeling
technology is freedom's other name when
—a meadowlark
comes sailing across my windshield
with breast shining yellow
and five notes pierce
the windroar like a flash
of nectar on mind,
gone as the country music swells up and drops
                    me wheeling down
            my notch of cement-bottomed sky
                    between home and away
and wanting
to move again through country that a bird
has defined wholly with song,
and maybe next time see how
            he flies so easy, when he sings.

What the Eagle Fan Says

(For the Voelkers and the Besses)

I strung dazzling thrones   of thunder beings
on a spiraling thread   of spinning flight,
beading dawn's blood   and blue of noon
to the gold and dark   of day's leaving,
circling with Sun   the soaring heaven
over turquoise eyes   of Earth below,
her silver veins,   her sable fur,
heard human relatives   hunting below
calling me down,   crying their need
that I bring them closer   to Wakonda's ways,
and I turned from heaven   to help them then.
When the bullet came,   it caught my heart,
the hunter's hands   gave earth its blood,
loosed our light beings,   let us float
toward the sacred center   of song in the drum,
but fixed us first   firm in song-home
that green light-dancers   gave to men's knives,
ash-heart in hiding where   deer-heart had beat,
and a one-eyed serpent   with silver-straight head
strung tiny rattles   around white softness
in beaded harmonies   of blue and red—
lightly I move now   in a man's left hand,
above dancing feet   follow the sun
around old songs   soaring toward heaven
on human breath,   and I help them rise.

Birch Canoe

Red men embraced   my body's whiteness,
cutting into me   carved it free,
sewed it tight   with sinews taken
from lightfoot deer   who leaped this stream—
now in my ghost-skin   they glide over clouds
at home in the fish's   fallen heaven.

In Chigger Heaven

We grew up crossing
the bluestem meadow full of flowers
in May, when butterflies were coming out to meet
the flowers at last as equals, like
equations that have found
their Einstein and can sip the nectar
of hyperspace at will,
and when also
were hatching out the tiny scarlet
chiggers, holding up their hooks
for rides toward heaven,
not on brilliant wings but into
the skin and making keratin cocktails
of huge paradisal monsters like us.
Well, *noblesse oblige*—
like angels, we
took them into eternity as far
as they were going, helping them
believe in Providence. Maybe
to angels,
when they come down to snuff
wild flowers of gratitude or skunks
of treachery, time is only
a chigger-bite they carry back to heaven,
or maybe souls
can't change until they've tapped into
red lasers pulsing under
the bright skin of stars. Maybe
every infinitesimal
eleven-dimensioned string
wiggles into a downy
angelic wing and flies to places
it does not see,
like scarlet chiggers on a redwinged
blackbird's epaulette, or like

the blackbird's feet not grasping,
within the wire it's on,
the good news from Jerusalem or
a quasar at this universe's edge. To lie down
in green pastures and get up
as Providence—
that is, with chiggers—
may not be a sign
of misspent youth, but I wonder who
is itching with these words,
within what space and time.

Close Encounters

1.

We of the Osage Nation have come,
as the Naming Ceremony says,
down from the stars.
We sent ahead
our messengers to learn
how to make our bodies,
to make ourselves a nation,
find power to live, to go on,
to move as the sun rises and never fails
to cross the sky into the west
and go down in beauty into the night,
joining the stars once more
to move serenely across the skies
and rise again at dawn, letting
the two great shafts of light beside the sun
become white eagle plumes in the hair
of children as we give their names.

When we came down, our messengers
encountered beings
who let us take their bodies
with which we live into the peaceful days.
We met the Thunder, and the Mountain Lion,
the Red Bird, and the Cedar Tree,
Black Bear, and Golden Eagle.
As eagles, we came down,
and on the red oak tops
we rested, shaking loose with our weight
great showers of acorns, seeds
for new oaks, and our daily bread.

The leaves were light and dancing and
we saw, through the trees,
the sun caught
among leaves moving
around its light. It was
the leaves, we saw,
those light beings, who raised
as they danced the heavy
oak-trunks out of earth,
who gathered the wind and sunlight,
the dew and morning into timbered
lodges for the sun and stars.

And so, of course, we sang.
Nothing's lighter than leaves, we sang,
ghost-dancing on the oak tree as the spirit moves,
and nothing heavier than the great
sun-wombing red oak which their dancing
in time has raised up from this earth where we
came down as eagles.
It will not end, we sang,
in time our leaves of paper will
be dancing lightly, making a nation of
the sun and other stars.

2.

Coming down to Las Vegas as
a passenger on Frontier Airlines is
a myth of another color. At the Stardust Inn, deep
within that city of dice and vice and Warhead Testing,
I was to give a paper
to the Rocky Mountain Modern Language Association
on Trickster Tales.

I gave it, and
I got out solvent, astonished,
and all but stellified
on wings of flame—like Elijah
or Geoffrey Chaucer in the House of Fame, up
up into the stars above Lake Mead, and I looked down
into the lake's twinkling heaven
and thought back to the many-splendored
neon and krypton lights of Las Vegas
that throbbed with the great lake's power.
I remembered the dead rapids and waterfalls
drowned in Glen Canyon and Lake Mead,
thought of those bodies of
water swollen so huge that earth itself
quivers with constant
small tremors from them—
and there, looking up at me with his
Las Vegas eyeball, was the Trickster Monster,
flashing with lightning from his
serpents of copper lifted up on crossbars—
but then I remembered how
among the streaked and painted bluffs that surround
Las Vegas I saw the October dawn come streaked
and painted down from the eastern skies to brighten
the walk from my Travelodge over the street
to a vacant lot under
its desert willows
where lived a wren, some vivid orange flowers
papery on thornleaved stems hugging the sand,
and one empty billfold
with its credit cards spread around a sole
identity card that pictured
a security guard from San Diego,
that naval base there.
I turned the billfold in

to the motel clerk, the wren
pleaded innocent and flew away like me,
and when I got the orange flower
back to St. Louis and put it into
a glass of water, it turned that water
to pungent amber then wilted as if
I'd killed it with kindness.
—That Trickster, he always carries
lost identity cards and desert flowers,
and finds himself
surrounded by dawn.

And so I sang
how the white sails of Columbus, of
Cortez and the Pilgrims, brought
this krypton iris here and made
the desert bloom,
how they raised
the great light-sculptured houses
of cards and dice on sand—
I sang how
the rainbow ghosts of waterfalls
are pulsed into the sockets of
Las Vegas lights and flash in crimson, green,
gold and violet its humongous word,

VACANCY

VACANCY

up to the dancing
stars.

Wazhazhe Grandmother

—*I-ko-eh, tha-gthi a tho.*
[*Ho-e-ga*, literally "bare spot": the center of the forehead of the
mythical elk . . . a term for an enclosure in which all life takes on
bodily form, never to depart therefrom except by death. . . . the
earth which the mythical elk made to be habitable by separating it
from the water . . . the camp of the tribe when ceremonially pitched
. . . life as proceeding from the combined influences of the cosmic
forces.
— FRANCIS LA FLESCHE, *A Dictionary of the Osage Language*, 1932]

They chose their allotted land
out west of the Agency
at the prairie's edge,
where the Osage Hills begin they built
their homestead, honeymooned there
near Timber Hill,
where Bird Creek meanders in
from the rolling grassy plains with their prairie chicken
dancing in spring,
built in a timbered hollow where deer came down
at dusk with the stars
to drink from the deep pools
near Timber Hill
and below the
waterfall that seemed
so high to me the summer
when I was six and walked up near its clearness gliding
some five or six feet down from the flat
sandstone ledge to its pools;
she called it in Osage, *ni-xe,*
the dark water turning into
a spilling of light
was a curtain clear and flowing, under
the blue flash of a kingfisher's diving
into the pool above the falls

and his flying up
again to the dead white branch of his willow—
the whole place was so quiet,
the way Grandma was quiet,
it seemed a place to be still,
seemed waiting for us,
though no one lived there by then
since widowed during the war she'd moved
to the place south of Pawhuska,
and why we had driven down there from Timber Hill, now, I
can't quite remember—
was it a picnic, or some kind
of retreat or vacation time
out of the August heat of Pawhuska?
The pictures focus sharp-edged:
a curtain of dark green ivy ruffled
a bit by breeze and water beside
the waters falling there
and a dirt road winding red and rocky
across tree-roots, along which, carefully,
my mother eased our rumbling Buick Eight
in that Depression year when Osage oil
still gushed to float us on into
a happy future—
but whether I dreamed, or saw real things in time,
their road, their house, the waterfall back in the woods
are all
at the bottom of Lake Bluestem now,
because Bird Creek,
blessed with a dam,
is all Psyched out
of its snaggly, snaky self into a
windsparkling lake
whose deep blue waters are now
being piped into Pawhuska pure and drinkable,

filling with blue brilliance municipal pools
and sprinkling the lawns to green or pouring freshets
down asphalt gutters to cool the shimmering
cicada-droning fevers of August streets
even as
in Bird Creek's old channel under Lake Bluestem,
big catfish
grope slowly in darkness
up over the sandstone ledge of the drowned
waterfall, or
scavenge through the ooze of
the homestead and along the road where
an Osage bride and her man came riding one special day
and climbed down from the buggy in all their
best finery
to live in their first home.

Ponca War Dancers

1.

When Uncle Gus came to visit
     his nephew Buck's new wife,
     she was so polite and nice
     he really liked her very much,
but she talked directly to him,
     and that's not right
     in Ponca ways—
still, he just ignored her efforts
     at conversation,
     or spoke to Buck for her to overhear,
until one day with Buck at work
     she asked Uncle Gus to carry groceries
     into the house—
     and that was when he quietly
     left Kansas City,
though she could never figure out
     till finally Aunt Jewell had to explain.

2.

He was the greatest of Ponca dancers,
     yet when he came to see
     some of my white uncles
and they went off to drink,
     how come I never understood
     he was a champion,
     but saw a heavy-bellied
     quick talking man
     that kids swarmed round,
full of jokes and laughter,
     never seemed to brawl or argue—
     till at the Osage dances one June when he
     was sixty-something

I saw him dance for the first time
and everybody got quiet
except to whisper
"the champion"—
and here came Uncle Gus
potbellied but quick-footed went
twirling and drifting,
stomping with the
hawkwing a-hover then
                          leaping
    spinning light as
        a leaf in a whirlwind,
                the anklebells shrilling, dancing
    the Spirit's dance
        in a strange land where
    he had gone and fasted
                          and found his vision
        to lead his people
but had nowhere to lead them except
                into white ways—
                    so here he danced
        in Wahkondah's circle,
            drum at the center,
                    the old songs being sent up
        in the brilliant bugfilled light
            among bleachers and tourists
        and the grave, merry faces
    Osage and Ponca, Otoe and Delaware,
        Quapaw and Omaha, Pawnee Comanche and Kaw,
    who saw what he was doing
        and how he did it well even when
    to the white eyes watching he was
an old Indian slowing down
        and between dances going
                to have another slug of

            hell, maybe Old Crow or even
                Canadian Club,
good enough for the Champion.

        3.

A year after Wounded Knee in Seventy-Three
    it was his memorial feast they held
down in Ponca City, the auditorium
we had to drive around to find
    (White Eagle grounds being used
    for another Ponca funeral then),
and I drove in to it with the sons and daughters
    of his sister Jewell,
            all strong in AIM,
                and some just back from
a confrontation down in Pawnee where they tried
to keep some AIM supporters from being evicted
out of their own houses—drove
with my cousins Carter and Craig and Dwain and Serena,
    none of them underground yet
            from Wounded Knee, nor
the helicopters sweeping
    the Okie hills once more for them as they would be
next year, as back in the Thirties the marshals
    in V-8 Fords had swept the back roads hunting
their dad, Uncle Woody, when he was hiding
out down by Buck Creek on bootlegging charges,
    catching catfish to eat but letting
        the Big Bass get away—Jesus, think
of that "Gatsby" bunch in the Thirties making bootleg stuff
up in Canada, and running it down to Boston, making
    their family's fortune so big while Uncle Woody
was facing jail for the same white lightning—and think

                                            [25]

how in the Nineteen Seventies those same "Gatsbys"
had got so rich they'd be marrying off into
    some British titled family,
about the time when Uncle Woody
            was just thumbing his rides along
cross-country highways from California eastward to join
    his sons at Wounded Knee—but that's
American history for you, and here on the way to Uncle Gus's
    memorial feast,WE weren't in trouble,
            just driving all crowded up
                in my old Dart,
with Stephanie from Third Mesa, with Mickey
                from Pine Ridge, with Geronimo
    and Big Jim Jump and Mary Ann teaching us
            Cherokee and all of us singing
Forty-Nine songs on our way to the feast—
        Let's all go up to Porcupine,
        Indians dance in the summertime,
        We will dance the Forty-Nine,
            Heyehehyoahyo . . .
Me, I could never get the
Right number of yo's and hey's and drive straight too—
Besides, that damn state patrolman was tailgating us
        just waiting for a "traffic violation"
                to nail these Militant Indians good—
but we had put the wine in our trunk so they could not
    possibly get us for Driving with
    Open Bottle—
                still, it was getting dark and I of course
        was scared shitless wondering
                if we'd get shot
        by troopers or by FBI
                or maybe by some skins that had been
        lied to or bought or blackmailed,
but Carter and Craig and Buck were cool as a

hawk looking down
	from riding the wind to where bluejays
	are calling it names—
"Hey, Mike," Buck said, "Ever time I see you somebody's
	getting ready to shoot us, like out
		at Sunset Lake in '52,
			up in Wounded Knee last year,
				now here in Ponca country—
why don't you ever come see us when things
	are peaceful, so we can
			talk about old times?"
"Aw shit, Buck," I said, watching the grim
	trooper in my rearview mirror,
		"I only hope we live to talk
			when these times are old!"

But near the auditorium, the trooper
turned off,and we all pulled in safe,
piled out and went in to Uncle Gus's feast,
	where all the Ponca and Osage women
		had fixed the frybread, boiled beef (sure tastes like
			slow elk, we all said), lots of fruit
				and Jello and all,
	and we ate until our bellies
They'd brought the Osage drum
	out of mourning to honor Uncle Gus,
		and the Osage War Dancers
		had come to dance for him;
			then when the Hethushka singers
			sang the McDonald song all his
nephews and nieces danced slowly round
		tall and straight and proud.
			It was a good time there and we gave
all that we could away, blankets and
	shawls and canned hams, even

the big box of groceries won
in the drawing we gave away,
                        the only trouble
broke out when Buck's woman got mad at his flirting
with someone else and she took
                his gun and hid it,
                        but she came and told me
where it was
                and we got it back—nobody
got shot or busted that night,
        and toward the end of the dancing an old
                cowboy wandered over
        to where I stood behind the bleachers'
        he watched the war-dancers a while
                then said to me offhand,
"They're good,
        but they won't ever be as good
                        as Gus McDonald."
I told Carter what he'd said
        when we sat later back in a corner
                near closing time in a Ponca City bar,
watching the door
        and wondering who was sober enough
to stay on the right side back to Stillwater that night.
        "How about that," Carter said quietly,
        "Uncle Gus was the best all right.
                —Mike, they'll nail me some time or other
for Wounded Knee. I know it, I'm prepared long since.
        But I'm back with my people now."
Well, they nailed him
        next year all right, caught him
                in Chicago finally,
hell, we were glad when we heard he hadn't
                        been murdered,
        even glad when we heard he'd serve

his three years in a Federal pen.
We laughed about that being in INDIANa,
    were kind of surprised when they shifted him
    over to Springfield MO, and of course
it was not too bad, he only got three years
    for disarming (allegedly) a postal inspector
        inside Wounded Knee:
neither snow nor sleet nor Ponca warriors
    should stay the appointed rounds of those
    who bring junk mail to advertise
    how to become Horatio Alger on
the Pine Ridge Reservation, man.

    4.

Shongeh-ska: that was Uncle Gus's name.
His niece Serena put it on her Indian crafts shop run
        by her and her husband Mike
                for as long as people would buy
                    and run, by God,
of the people
        by the people
                and for the people
who shall not perish from the earth,
        not even if they have to use
such European words as these
        to keep the Ponca ways together:
                not being much of a warrior myself,
                    cousins, Aunt Jewell,
I've set down this winter-count for a kind
        of memorial song
                to *Shongeh-ska*, one
of the greatest of Ponca dancers,
                to dance once more.

We know that even
where Poncas are in prison
the songs are with them,
how can the bars stop singing
inside their heads?
For those who saw him dance,
and learned from him the way,
he is dancing still.
Come to White Eagle in the summer time,
Indians dance in summer time—
he is back with his people now.

Over by Fairfax, Leaving Tracks

The storm's left
    this fresh blue sky, over
Salt Creek running brown
    and quick, and a huge tiger
        swallowtail tasting the brilliant
orange flowers beside our trail.
    Lightning and thunder've spread
        a clean sheet of water over
these last-night possum tracks
    straight-walking like a dinosaur in
        soft mud, and next to these we've
left stippled tracks from soles made
    in Hong Kong, maybe with Osage oil.
Lawrence and Wesley pick blue-speckled flints
along our path, one Ponca boy
    in braids, one Osage
        in cowboy hat.
        Over the blue Pacific, green Atlantic we
have come together here: possum's
the oldest furred being in this New World,
    we're newest in his Old World.
Far older, though,
    and younger too, the tiger swallowtail has
gone sailing from those orange flowers to
    sky-blue nectar: the wild morning
    glories
will spring up where she's touched, marking
    her next year's trail.
Makes me wonder,
    if archaeologists should ever dig these prints
with possum's here, whether they'll see
the winged beings who moved
in brightness near us, leaving no tracks except
    in flowers and
        these winged words.

Getting Across

Hanging
      out under the bridge
      by fingertips and a toe
      between ledge and girder, high
      over deep water and thinking,
      I can't swim,
      unreachable by the older boys
      who've made it across, he watches
      the steelblue flashing of wings
      and chestnut bellies of barnswallows
shooting and swirling around him,
      below him,
      a two-foot gar's black shadow
      in the greenbrown water, and before
      he has weakened lets
      the toe slip gently and swings
      down like a pendulum, hand over
hand along the girder to where
the others perch
      on the concrete ledge,
      has kicked up his right leg onto
the ledge and is
      pulled to its safety, can look back
      now at the swallow's easy
      curve upwards, its
      flutter and settling
gently into the cup
of feather-lined mud there nestling
      on the shining girder's side
      where he has passed his death.

Pure Country

1.

Pick and shovel dug the privy-hole square
down into orange clay
under the garden's loam,
a foot of black soil,
two feet of pebbly grayness,
then clay and the pale harsh rocks
in shovelfuls grating up
to splat on the loose-sided mound
next to the pit,
then shoveling the mound out over
the garden soil around it
and shoving, levering the white clapboard privy
on rollers until it was perched above
the eight-foot pit
on steel pipes,
plunking the loam
and clay around its bottom edges firm,
going in, stamping, rocking, leveling, and seeing
that the door would swing
open, and close, and the hook to latch it
worked just fine.

2.

The water-well pierced down and down through loam,
through clay, through pebbles and
bedrock by pick and sledges and
spike and shovel, buckets on
ropes to take the dirt up
then setting flat rocks atop each other round
and around its roundness when the water began
to rise and fill and darken; rocking in
the sides completely, sanding

the bottom over,
how deep? twenty feet
to the splash, twelve feet that the bucket
would sink on down slowly, pause
and settle, until a pull
would bring it dreaming upward so it broke
the darklit surface with a Floosh!
and like a soul in flesh grew heavy
but rose to the straining hands
full of light-sparkles shaking
and fresh rock-tasting water spilling
back down the dark echoes to where
it shivered alive with breathing.

3.

In the privy after five years or so
bluegreen bottle-flies humming
around the toilet-hole, the loose newspapers
brown-stained and musty with the news
of last year's football, wars
and sermon topics, down in
the acrid darkness webs sticky
in masses, sparkling here and there
bluegreenly with the shells
of flies sucked dry and the oily
gleam of black widows waiting
below and to the side of
the naked bottoms there on the hole above them,
flies drawn by the smell,
spiders after the flies,
filth rising to meet them.

4.

The year we moved the privy
from its old pit filled and stinking
to the new and fresh-dug one,
we shoveled earth into and over
the old one and stamped it quaking down,
but it did not let us off
untouched, the oldest of us missed
his footing when a pipe gave way and he slowly sank
up to his chest in the liquid stuff
before he could grab a rope,
and we pulled our grandfather up
with a heave, looked at each other's faces and
broke out laughing like hell and he—
without a single word even to swear, he looked
down at his dripping self for a minute and then
turned and walked silent along
the path to the well
stripping his clothes as he walked,
and at the well drew up the buckets full
of sun-bright water and moving away
poured it all over him, scrubbed
and poured and then soaped and poured and
scrubbed and poured
till he was clean in
the dry September day and walked
in the house and got clean clothes and came out
and we moved the privy on out
above its new-dug hole.

Cowboys and Indians

Yes, he was a good shot and rode a horse well,
herded cattle for big ranchers
sometimes, rented a little place and raised most
of the family's food when he could, lived on the edges
of towns or in the smallest ones—
a cheerful man,
would fix what broke; rent him a little house,
the fences and the yard would be
kept straight and friendly, 'yours' and 'mine' kept clear
but no doors locked, a visit always
welcomed and too short, would lift your spirits.
See, the movies
just never show how cowboys took
care of things, would doctor cows
and bale the hay, help with grandchildren,
have pockets full of mints or
dimes to give them when he came to visit.
Yes, they hugged his legs,
they knew a day's work didn't keep him
from driving down to see them in the evening.
The movies never show a cowboy's children might
marry an Indian's, his grandchildren crowd in close
to see the snake-eggs that he found
digging fence-holes that day.
White, soft-shelled,
translucent. His pocket knife would pierce
a leathery shell, its clear liquid spill down,
the small triangular head poke through,
a four-inch snakelet ooze on out,
minute forked tongue flickering; coiling,
nervous and quick.
Rattler or milksnake?
That was the question—maybe copperhead?

The point is, nothing ever kept him
from having other people firmly in mind.
He liked finding such things, but what
he liked most was bringing them
for kids to see. Yes, they'll see
the man who brought them; that is how
he stays with them.
No, he wasn't
John Wayne or Lorne Green. Oklahoma into
Hollywood does not go. Still, there are
other places. And where he has gone,
if anybody values neighbors they
are crowding round and seeing what he's brought
and glad to have it, too.
Mints, dimes, snake-eggs.
A good man.

Communing Before Supermarkets

—It's probably because we were always trying
to have enough money to eat
that I can taste and smell the truckloads
of summer that came by and sometimes
turned jouncing up the long
dirt lane from U.S. Sixty to our house—
they saw kids swarming out in the yard,
white house with a green roof and a big white
two-story garage, haybarn and cowbarn,
nothing around but meadow, no crops, no
rows of corn or hills of watermelons, a lot of hungry kids
that would be wanting what they were taking round
from their truck farms or orchards—
elephantine loads of melons, sometimes the light
green long ones, the striped ones, the dark
green cannonballs, incredible abundance,
or old swaying trucks loaded with bushels of peaches,
apples and apricots, with grapes and pears that I
remember. I wonder, now, where they came from—
over in Sand Creek Valley by the little town
in the Osage Hills, the hamlet really,
they called it Okesa where we
drove once: there we saw a hillside full
of orchards, berry bushes, the sandy bottomland shaggy
with watermelon vines where the great green melons rounded
heavy and warm on the loam—
it struck me staring from the car, how strange
that dirt does turn into their sweet crisp red flesh
and juice in the mouth, that those long vines
can draw the dark earth up and make it melons, and I said
to myself, how does the seed know to make
a watermelon and not an apricot. Then we had brought
our dimes and pennies for a summer's day, we took
the silver and the copper and we turned
them into two huge melons that the blond boy went casually

out into the field and pulled, just those we wanted,
he took our thirty cents and we—
I think we drove away back down to Sand Creek and in
the pebbly shallow ford we drove out in the water and killed
the engine and we took
the melons from the trunk and in the shallow ripples splashed
each other and the car, we washed the car, the melons,
we took them out onto the bank and sat
on a blanket spread across the grass and stuck
a great long butcher knife into the first green melon and it split,
it was so ripe it cracked almost before the knife
could cut it open, the red heart
looked sugar-frosted, dewy with juice and the pieces
broke to our fingers better than to knives,
in the mouth crisp and melting fragrant, spicy nearly,
as pieces of rind were scattered the ants reporting mountains of
manna climbed and swarmed and buried themselves in our leavings
as we stripped to shorts and underthings and waded down into
the deeper colder pool below the ford where the springs
welled slowly out from under the bouldery bank
at the bend, and swimming I thought,
now the melon is turning into me, and my sisters and brothers,
my mother and father and uncles and aunts and into the
ants feasting there on the melon-rinds,
and into the grass and the trees growing there, and into the dirt—
and Sand Creek is turning, this day is turning to night, so now
when we go home I'll remember and it will be turned
into words, and maybe sometime
it would all grow again a long way off, a long way into
the future, and that's what a few pennies and dimes can do
if you have them, a few seeds, a little rain where creekwaters rise,
and the whole world turns into food for all
the different beings in their times.

An Eagle Nation

For the Camp/Jump Brigades

You see, I remember this little Ponca woman
who turned her back to the wall and placed her palms
up over her shoulders flat on the wall
and bent over backwards and walked her hands down the wall
and placed them flat on the floor behind her back—that's
how limber she was, Aunt Jewell,
when I was a boy.
And FAST! you wouldn't BELIEVE how she could sprint:
when an Osage couple married, they would ask Aunt Jewell
to run for the horses for them.
Now she's the eldest in her clan, but still the fastest
to bring the right word, Ponca or English, sacred or
profane, whatever's needed to survive she brings it, sometimes in
a wheelchair, since her heart alarms
the doctors now and then. —So one bright day, we loaded
the wheelchair, and ourselves, and lots of chicken
barbecued and picnic stuff
into our cars and zoomed away
from Ponca City and White Eagle, *Southward Ho!*
To the Zoo! we said, *the Oke City Zoo—we'll picnic there!*
Grandchildren, see, they love the zoo,
and has she got GRANDchildren? well, maybe
one of her children knows how many, the rest of us
stopped counting years ago, so there were quite a few
with serious thoughts of chicken barbecue and we all rolled in
to the Zoo and parked, and we walked, scrambled, rolled,
we scuttled and sprinted—we used up all the verbs
in English, she'd have to get those Ponca words
to tell you how we made our way,
but somehow we ALL of us got in, and found
the picnic tables, and we feasted there and laughed
until it was time to inspect the premises, to see just what
the children of Columbus had prepared for us.
Snow leopards and black jaguars, seals and dolphins, monkeys and

baboons, the elephants and tigers looked away
thinking of Africa, of Rome, oceans, dinnertime, whatever—
and as for us, we went in all directions—
grandchildren rolled and bounced like marbles up and down
curved asphalt ways, played hide and seek, called me to look
at *camels* maybe. And then we were all
getting tired and trying to reassemble, when Casey
came striding back to where we were wheeling Aunt Jewell
and said, "Mom,
there's this eagle over here you should see,"
and we could tell it mattered. So we wheeled along
to this cage set off to itself with a bald eagle sitting,
eyes closed and statue-still,
on the higher perch inside, and there was a couple
standing up next to the cage and trying
to get its attention.
A nice white couple, youngish, the man
neatly mustached and balding, the woman
white-bloused and blondish. The man clapped hands
and clicked his tongue and squeaked, and whistled. The eagle
sat motionless. Casey wheeled Aunt Jewell
a little to the side. The man quit making noises. He
and the woman looked at each other, then us, then looked away.
There was a placard on the cage's side that said:
This bald eagle was found wounded, and
although its life was saved, it will never fly again,
so it is given this cage to itself.
Please do not feed him.
Aunt Jewell, from her wheelchair, spoke in Ponca to him,
so quietly that I could hardly hear
the sentences she spoke.
Since I know only
a few words of Ponca, I can't be sure
what she said or asked, but I caught the word

[41]

Kahgay: Brother, she said.
The eagle opened his eyes and turned his head.
She said something else. He partly opened his beak
and crouched and looked head-on towards her,
and made a low shrill sound.
—The white couple were kind of dazed, and so was I.
I knew she was saying good things for us.
I knew he'd pass them on.
She talked a little more, apologizing for all of us, I think.
She put one hand up to her eyes and closed them for a while
till Casey handed her a handkerchief
and she wiped her eyes.
"I guess we're about ready to go now," Aunt Jewell said,
so we wheeled back to the cars, and we gathered all
the clan and climbed aboard
and drove from the Zoo downtown to where
the huge *Red Earth* powwow was going on, because
her grandson Wesley, Mikasi, was dancing there.
We hadn't thought Aunt Jewell's heart
was up to Zoo and Powwow in one day, but as usual she
knew better. THEY CHARGED ADMISSION, and that really
outraged my Ponca folks, for whom
a powwow should be free. Worse than that,
the contest DANCERS had to pay a fee.
"That's not our way," Aunt Jewell said.
But once inside we found our way,
wheelchair and all, up to the higher tiers,
where we and thousands of Indian people looked down
to the huge Arena floor where twelve drums
thundered and fourteen hundred dancers spun and eddied round,
and dancing in his wolfskin there
was Mikasi where Casey pointed, and we saw
his Grampa Paul Roughface gliding, with that eagle's calm he has,
and I saw how happy Casey and Mike were then

that their eldest son was dancing down there, and I felt
what the drum did for Aunt Jewell's heart and ours, and she told us
of seventy years ago when she was a little girl and her folks
would load the wagons up there in White Eagle and go
and ford the Arkansas—no bridge nearby—and cross
into Osage country and drive all day
and camp at night on the prairie and then drive on
to the Grayhorse Osage Dances, or those in Pawhuska even.
I remembered how Uncle Woody Camp had told me
of going to the Osage dances later and seeing her
for the first time and asking:
Who is that beautiful Ponca girl over there?
and someone said, *Oh, that's McDonald's daughter,*
and they met that way. And he and Uncle Dwain would tell
of the covered wagon in which they also rode,
my Irish and Scotch-Irish mother's folks, from Missouri out
to the Kansas wheat harvest after their mother died,
and then on down to the Osage Reservation in Oklahoma,
where mules were needed, and our grandfather hauled the bricks
to build the oil-boom agency town of Pawhuska where million-dollar
lease sales, and the Osage Dances, were held.
So I was thinking how the eagles soared,
in their long migration flights, over all these places,
how they looked down on the wagons moving
westward from Missouri, eastward from Ponca lands
to meet in Pawhuska, how all the circles
had brought us into this Oklahoma time and what
had passed between cage and wheelchair before
we mounted up to view on this huge alien floor the long-ago drum
in its swirling rainbow of feathers and
bells and moccasins lifting up here
the songs and prayers from long before cars or wagons,
and how it all has changed and the ways are strange but
the voices still

are singing, the drum-heart
still beating here, so whatever the placards on
their iron cages may have to say, we the people,
as Aunt Jewell and Sun Dancers say,
are an EAGLE NATION, now.

Dragon-watching in St Louis
—for Stephen, Geoffrey, Vanessa, Lawrence

It would have been a dragon, this monstrous jet,
two hundred years ago, to father and little boy
come out for a stroll, had they seen it go screeching down
into the sunset with sweptback wings downglinting
as their words rose like drowned twigs from a stream,
the little boy exclaiming, the father agreeing.
They would have fled in terror what we take in stride
since we live near an airport and have rendezvoused
with sun and horizon here too often to fear
that this great beast might shatter, his smoky fires dim
the park, touched by the sun's last shining, we've come to see.

By the dark-mortared wall, whose chalk-white stones protect
this place from the roaring fuming freeway beneath us,
we can look far over its asphalt and across suburban roofs
at how the jetplane now small and tranquil is sinking,
winking the ruby of its landing light, in the last
seconds before it touches the earth beneath our horizon—
and we listen until it's touched safely down like the sun,
till silence tells us it's landed, as darkness tells us
that the trillion hydrogen bombs of our sun eyeballing space
to light and warm us this day have held their peace,
as firmness tells feet that the earth, whose sensitive crust's
light quiver would bury us in our buildings, now smoothly
turns on appointed rounds as it brings this smoky city
gliding through sunset into starlit night, as that dazzle of
cars weaving through traffic snarls and homing on supper
            smells
tells us it's time to be strolling back home on the safe
sidewalks of this suburb—where bears and panthers, flood and
fire and that fearful monster the Wild Osage, whose blood
runs in our veins, ranged these savage woodlands hundreds
of years ago, before the walks were made safe for us to enjoy
this zoo of smoky dragons now swarming from our best brains.

That Lightning's Hard to Climb
—For Thelma Louise Camp

—Struck down?
Good Lord, we'd always be
climbing that tall catalpa tree—
its leaves our money, its long bean-pods
cigars, and all of May
we swung and taunted in high
danger and falling blossoms among those great
heart-shaped leaves where a loud beating
of raindrops made us, out on bending
almost-breaking limbs, reaching for nectar
in purple-streaked blossoms with gold stamens, feel
sheltered and vulnerable, seeing
how blue sky looked among
sun-lucent leaves as we hung waiting until
bright lines of rain came sweeping
down over us from the leafy hills above
our bluestem meadow and made us
see how the scissortails had placed
their nest beneath a tent of tilting leaves that the wind
kept parting above
 their nestlings, and how
the swaying giant held them in its arms as
the flashing giant glanced in
flooding silver down on them and on
their long-tailed mother sitting patient
and streaming off half-opened wings the dancing
spatter, and when
it had gone there was all the twinkle
and diamond flashing in the meadow, the ring and
whistle of robin, of orioles and
redwing blackbird sprinkling again the sunburst
tree in bloom from whose tip
the scissortails towering and inter-
weaving challenges could veer and dip and zoom
up and up, shrieking *treep. tree-eeee-EEP!* building

a musical tree to sing from—
while down below the trunk for us rose solid
from our twilit lawn, a safe base
for wood-tag runners as the dark filled up
with lightning
bugs, stars and cries of
the children running among
the trees while grownups watched from the
gloominous porch, talking of old
and happy faroff things
and laughter long ago—
so now the one
more storm has set blossoms
of fire exploding, now
the Lightning U-Haul has swung down and transported
our half-way house,
our swaying path
to the sky whose fall
seems to have saved our house
is gone, and only
some green shoots with their heart-shaped leaves
now mantle where the
living tree once stood.

And Don't Be Deaf to the Singing Beyond

Ed al cantar di là, non siate sorde:
Angel in Flames to DANTE, Purgatorio 27.12

You never could tell what my deaf Uncle Arthur heard.
That Sunday when the black storm-cloud came at us,
He sat there churning butter by the bedroom window.
We saw this strange cloud way off west on the hills,
A little dark funnel with specks dancing round it.
"That's only a big whirlwind," he said with a smile.
Well, pretty soon we saw the specks were trees,
We heard this rumble like freight trains on a trestle,
But Uncle Arthur was deaf and wouldn't believe us.
We ran like hell to the car and drove off east—
When hail and rain came blasting after to blind us,
He just sat there in the window, churning away.
Of course the storm passed before we got to the school
And ran down steps to stand in its flooded cellar—
So, wet up to our knees, we drove back home.
When we got in, he had two pounds of butter
All worked, salted, and molded onto dishes.
The funnel had passed a half-mile north and west,
Its swath—a quarter-mile wide of leveled blackjacks—
Went up and over the valley's northern rim.
We drove up north to find out who'd been killed.
Out in the dirt yard of their paintless four-room house
Our Assembly of God friends were standing unharmed.
"We knelt and prayed, God turned his wrath aside,"
Their mother said. Who knows which tasted sweeter,
That Jersey butter from Uncle Arthur's churn,
Or the name of God in Mrs. Parks's mouth?
I still get peeved, thinking of what missed them
So close they saw the lightning up in its blackness,
And what we missed, down in that scorpion-filled cellar.
Well, when my Uncle Arthur died, years later,
A migrant Okie in Porterville, California,

My Aunt Jewell, his brother Woody's wife,
Saw him collapse there with his coronary,
And when she ran up, he lay there on his back,
Turned his eyes to her, smiled, closed them, was dead.
"He was so deaf," she said, "and he saw my mouth
    Just calling and calling, and seemed to think it was funny."

Looking Before and After

Under the new pond-dam
a trickle
like a spring fills
old pools among
the button-bushes where you
step between rusting bedsprings
blackberry vines
persimmon trees & wild grape tangles and
where the matted grass gives
way to shining there is
footdeep water so clear that over
its brown silt bottom, haloes dazzle round the
shadows trailed by water-striders in
their spindly-crooked dimpling across its
springy surface so
each bright-edged darkness glides up to
and over brown crawdads bulldozing through
the mud-dust,
and see, one shadow-cluster is
a gliding skull whose two
great eyes stare above its
nose and three black teeth,
it wanders,
lunges, glides,
spins upside down and turns
to butterfly! that stops precisely underneath
an image of white larkspur nodding upon
the water's surface so it seems
that dimly there
among cruising crawdads a
butterfly of shadows tastes
sweet light again.

Aunt Jewell as Powwow Princess

I was AGHAST at what I saw,
I've got no way of seeing things like that.
Felt kind of like I was sitting on a rock
and suddenly I saw a label on it
that said, URANIUM.
Sometimes it's super-real, you see into things,
I mean you see
what isn't there, but yet it makes
the things you CAN see have a different meaning.
I think for some Indian people just
like for physicists who figure how
to look inside some distant star, it's possible
to see how each thing, deep inside,
is something else, all made of crazy things
they may give crazy names,
quarks or whatever they may choose.
Well hell, for instance right
here in that word "aghast" which I just used, there lives
a "ghost"—because one thousand years ago, inside
those Anglo-Saxon warriors, the soul
that spoke and danced, they didn't call that
a SPIRIT but a GAST—so when they said AGHAST,
they meant something was walking in their SOUL.
So after all, maybe it's just as good to say
"Ghost Dance," as "Spirit Dance," the way
Americans say it, speaking
of what the people did who are called,
because of Columbus, INDIANS. Maybe
inside this English word INDIAN
there is a GHOST that haunts
all English-speakers, even in these words.
But here's the story: across the Mississippi from St. Louis,
there at Cahokia Mounds—
where we were dancing for

that Powwow-time
with Evelyne and her Comanche family,
who now are with Aunt Jewell and
our Ponca family as
an Eagle Nation, gathered by the passing
within their tepee of the Pipe among us—I sat one night
on a folding chair as Bob and Evelyne's sons
were dancing the Eagle Dance, and heard
Aunt Jewell tell me a story, that
September of her eighty-first year, of what she'd seen
under the first full moon
in August at a Sun Dance on the Rosebud. She said
they'd put the pole up in the night
under a huge moon, and then
the elders warned them, while the dancers there
were coming out in the Spirit Light to dance, of what
they might be seeing, and how
to understand, be calm, to hear
the strong-heart cries of warriors and
to know there were so many
of the Old People who would want
to come into the circle and dance, but now
they would be taken care of.
And then she heard their cries and saw
among the shadowy dancers spinning there
so many others just outside the arbor crowding in
long lines from where
the moon had risen—but they WERE
all right, she could see, without exactly
SEEING—
inside, she KNEW. I listened
to what she said, and at first
I only thought she was saying
how powerful the Sun Dance is, but then I saw—
I remembered how that afternoon

Earl Fenner came out from the drum and spoke
with our emcee Dale Besse, then went back
and started a song, and
Aunt Jewell said, LISTEN, and I said I heard
them singing KAH-GEH, "brother," and I looked at her
but she said firmly LISTEN to the WORDS,
and finally I heard: SHON-GEH-SKAH,
White Horse, Uncle Gus's name, they sang.
So then I understood
why she was telling about the Sun Dance: it was because
that afternoon she'd seen—without my saying anything—
that I was worried because I had just seen,
myself, under the half-moon in the daylight skies
there at Cahokia where the great city
of Indian people once had been,
her brother dancing, Uncle Gus,
who left us twenty years before,
and I don't see such things, but I saw him there
twice, dancing with
the hawk's wing he carried—
and now this evening, when the lights were on
and a half-moon golden in the west
above what might become
a thunderstorm, she told me, "Sonny,
this year after we were at Crow Dog's
we went to another Sun Dance too. I want to tell you
just a little about it,
we want to watch these
Eagle Dancers now, but soon
we'll find a time and talk about it,
and you can write it down."
So I remembered, then, how calm
Uncle Gus's face was when he danced,
there on the north side of our circle, how still
and fierce with understanding,

the way he always was.
And I felt good.
They'd brought us in,
that afternoon,
for the first Gourd Dance,
the women with green willow branches, behind
the Eagle Staff the Voelkers made for our Center,
and it felt good. And after supper
hundreds of Harley Davidsons came rumbling in,
great burly bearded bikers, some with skulls
on the gleaming quiet thunder of their machines,
and women bikers, some straight up cool
and distant, others grinning
with license plates like SASI-1—
and one of our Board Members, Charlotte Pipestem,
Otoe and ex-Marine, rode in on the pillion
behind a huge man—all the bikers
were packing bags and boxes
of groceries and supplies
to give the American Indian
Center of Mid-America for
our Food Pantry where the people
are given food and things when they come in—
maybe five hundred Harley Davidsons, mostly
with two people on them, men, women and little kids,
they turned in off the highway
and rode around the arbor set up and covered
with its green willow branches in
a great circle under those ancient mounds,
the bikers came in on their beautiful machines
the way the warriors used to ride
their horses in,
and at the East where the dancers
would bring the Eagle Staff in, Evelyne
and the Head Singer, her brother Rusty,

[54]

and the Head Man Dancer Warren Sovo, and
a lot of us, Gourd Dancers, one ex-Ranger, took
with thanks the food those bikers brought, set
the plastic and paper bags and boxes down
in a great overflowing heap beside the Arbor,
and rumbled off, I thought
into the wild
American yonder,
and that felt good, we saw for now
there's food for the elders and for
the children, for all the people, what they have
will be a feast—
and I thought,
well, now that's done, but it wasn't,
then Rusty and the singers and the dancers
called those bikers back into the Circle
and they came
on foot, over four hundred strong, and stood
around the Drum
while the Singers sang
an Honor Song for them,
and we dancers stood
behind them in the Circle,
all the spectators stood, and the song was sung,
and I did not see
Uncle Gus again that evening as the moon
was being covered by new clouds—
which after the Closing Song when the Staff
was posted sent a few small drops,
and on the way home, after
we'd passed beside the Arch,
just as we turned onto Delmar for home,
briefly
came down as a heavy rain.

When Earth Brings

For Joy and Daisy, grandmothers; for Simon, grandfather; for Rainy Dawn and Chris, parents; for Krista Rae, child; and for all our relatives.

When earth brings the sun
into deep translucent
morning around us, when stars go quietly into
blue air behind him, we know
they are telling us:
Grandchildren, here is one of us,
we have arranged for you to see
the world you have been given on this day
by the clear brilliance of
our brother only, at this time,
but we are here, we have not gone away,
the earth will bring us back to you,
return us to each other and you will see
with our little sister's light, and all of ours,
how you move always among our many worlds,
the light and darkness we are given that
we give to you.
Dawn
is a good word to tell you
how children come into a world
again and again and how grandparents see ahead
in the blue dazzle where
a rainy light descends upon the earth,
where light comes back into the children's eyes with word
of how the earth meets heaven and how, one special time,
each child will look into the rain that lives
again on earth in a small pool and say:
I see myself, I see the stars,
now light and water give me back again
the world and heaven in which I live
and move and have my being,
here where the earth has brought
us everything, this day.

In the Suburbs

A Mandala of Sorts

Sparrows twittering, rain cold and dim—
This windless October eve the dusk comes down
As through endless depths, and settles slowly,
Recoiling on itself, among dark branches
Of elm trees where rain gleams like iron
Around robins hopping nervous as minnows,
Setting out, this night, through the mist and rain.

Out by the street-crossing a lamp flares on,
Loosens white house-walls from the swaying darkness
Like lotus-petals to the lamp's electric jewel,
The corner houses, black-backed, where neighbors
Will sleep in the dazzled night, locked in whiteness,
Sleep and live, deep in their jeweled lotus.

I don't know how they live. Here at the edge
Of lamplight I can hear the low cries of birds leaving
And southward flying, down the edge of day,
Its bloodred circle where the spinning earth
Is stained with sunset, or the rose of dawn
Petals its dust with momentary bloom—

And I watch go riding down the gutter a feather
Spinning and twinkling, left by one of those birds
Whirled behind summer down the earth's tilting
Into the dawn, or across dark seas to shores
Hushed by their singing, where sunburned lovers lie
Among stars at dusk, and watch the gold moon rise.

In the Changing Light

Brimming the trees with song
they flood July, spill over into
August pulsing lovecries,
cicadas here—one that
our cat brought me lay, legs folded
neatly, on clear wings as on a shroud, green
and white, fizzing now and then,
but when I threw it spread
wings and zagged in a wide curve into
the sweetgum tree where presently
its dry buzzsaw whined for some
significant other to auger down
into dark dense earth and gnaw at
the roots of things,
sans eyes, sans wings, sans
song for seventeen years or so.

As daylight sharpens, deer slip back
into the woods. I wonder what a deer,
when danger grows too bright,
makes of a world whose darker,
truer memories in ear
and nose must solve the dazzle of
our alien eyes, more surgical
at stripping off its cover, at masking selves
as downwind leaves.
I've read somewhere the claim, by computer people,
that pain cannot be felt
until self-consciousness
has been achieved, and they had programmed in
that level, so they said, of artificial pain.
In A. R. Luria's book *The Mind*
of a Mnemonist, the man infallibly
remembered everything, but all perceptions
were unlike ours. Hearing, he tasted: sweet, bitter,

salty; heard neon colors; rough or silky, icy or
bloodwarm words: laid them like eggs aside on streets
his memory walked stolidly along,
walked back to get them when he needed to.
—Forgot, once, a word;
had set it carefully beneath a lamp
whose bulb was burnt out.
Bud opens and
is marigold, bird touched
by sunlight sings,
mind thinks:
I am. Still,
as the old man put it, coming out
into the light we wawl
and cry. I wonder,
in this darklit galaxy,
how that song is heard.

Outside in St. Louis

Walking through the door
is easy when it is your home—
but then, how many doors
belong to you? In time,
none,
except the one where it turns dark
and timeless. —But
it keeps us entertained, the sidewalk does,
with lighted windows, spring flowers
and autumn leaves, playthings of children
to walk around, step over—left
at dinner time to go inside to smells of
food and dancing pictures
on television screens; and here,
outside,
the pigeons tilt above me on their way
to find loose grain in a feedstore loft:
two, with
rainbows on their necks, descend to
waddle and peck
at ash wings in the gutter. What,
I wonder, do they fly through,
                    among,
                              within? Me,
I hear the traffic, step
with caution from the curb—
they, inside the whisper of
a soft St. Louis rain, may hear
the ocean speaking: not just the long swells that lash
Pacific shores, but those that boom
on Hatteras, commune on their
subhuman channels with these pigeons' minds;
maybe the rumbling of Colorado thunderstorms
forecasts for them this weekend's weather—
even through rainclouds, light is polarized to

brilliantine their way; and though
their way back into everlasting spring's
not lighted up, as for
the tiny migrant warblers who fly the Atlantic non-stop,
by star-maps glittering in the
molecules of their genes, their history
is packed, rainproof and portable,
in sperm and ova, even
the lodestone that they home with's just
a speck of ferrite in their brain—
      my God, these rock-doves make
from our crumbs a feast, of our windowsills
their trysting-places, set their pullulating
nests into dark empty places warmed by
our wasted heat:
The Outside is
their home, its door the wind, sidewalks just
angelic parking lots—
      So when they do
come spiraling down to sidewalks with
their Aphrodisiac sigh of wings, I hear
Her giggling as
they strut and coo: *She* lets them love it on
the outside of
the street's many doors,
as I remind myself in passing daily over
the hard concrete within our here and now
into some other space and time.

What the Poet's Cottage in Tucson Said

(for Simon, Ofelia, Larry, Joy, Scott and all)

At your finger's touch   my turquoise flower
of fossil sunlight   flashes, you call
from mountain springs   bright spurts of water
that dancing boil   on its blue petals
crushed seeds, their life's   loss repaid
with offered words.   Watchful electrons
in copper wall-snakes   await your cue
to dance like Talking God   down from heaven
and bring Mozart's   melodies back,
pixel this world's   woe and wonder, but
through wind's eye you see   the sun rising
as creatures of earth   from heaven's darkness
open iris-nets to   the harsh light
of human mysteries,   your *here* and *now*,
needle points   where numberless
angels are dancing,   *always* and *everywhere*.

How the Songs Come Down

Mid-May and from this dark
window I see the bright
full moon and starry heavens and
a streetlamp mellow in the new oak
leaves come shining down on two
midnight walkers through fire-opal
glimmer and leaf-shadow gliding off
and on them walking mid-street, white
T-shirt wobbling with her breasts, he bulge-
bellied in Bermuda shorts; they glance
up at this unlit window as they pass
us here in darkness—did
they hear? she pulls
his head down to her mouth and they keep walking;
in the shadows
did she whisper, kiss him, bite or—?
They think, no doubt, they are observers, not observed:
It's true that even with this house
in darkness, they know more of what we inside have
been doing than do our
children sleeping just across the hall;
you have to know before senses make sense, before
their cobweb clues conduct you to the heart
or exit of the mystery; then the selves
walking in public streets or prone in their private houses
let
their facts spill through although they always hold
surprises back—like
beaverdams, a tangle of
memories in the molecules retain a part of
what passes only, and the long-dead
words touches smells keep time as
lovers hold each other in the tangle of
their private selves.

Out back, the mockingbird is singing
       fortissimo in the high catalpa's blossoms
by our back alley: how in hell
      such birds evolved who sing at night
           when owls are listening for
           the stir of mice on tiptoes
is more than I can see; and he not only dee-Jays
      his own commercials, he jukeboxes
           the songs of all the other birds except
           I think for owls,
and more yet, those are territorial songs he's belting out:
he's riding like a carefree singing cowboy
dream fences of those other birds who perch
      moonlit with heads tucked
           and dreaming of owls and caterpillars
while midnight moths are probing
      catalpa blossoms unharassed
           by owls or mockingbirds (although
those flitting bat-songs won't
      have missed their furry shapes).

Walking on Skye,
      far up the mountain
           stream, I saw
      where a cataract hustled down among
    great granite boulders how the
dull rock suddenly glistened when
the sun spilled through the clouds
    into a million small orb-webs
like mirrors set at every angle
    where breeze might bring them flies;
           all over, boulders sparkled
    with webs,
      like words,
           like pictures on

                              the retina, fish
in beaver-ponds or songs in
                              mockingbirds or light
in pinoak leaves,
                    like time fixed
        on Mayan orbstones in a tangled
                        wheel of beasts who tell,
        from fragments buried in mud, just when
                the sun will darken in
                        two hundred years. And up
where the streams of Skye begin,
        in the watershed pass I have walked in under
                wind-blowing mist and walked into
cloud-fringes trailing past my fingers and cool into
                        my face, have dropped back flat on
        the star-moss looking up into
                mist-faces moving
in silence over me as the rocks,
                the great house-sized crystals of
greyness with their luminous lichen
        eyes of bluegreen and their heathery senses
                                        watched
mist-beings of my body flowing past them; to
        the rocks my passing was at near the speed
                of light, my hands were quarks that touched
        them as I climbed across the earth's
                eyeball, my feet a mere experiment that brought
me to them, whether a success or whether they had need of
        tensor calculus to relate my brown.
nylon rain-pants made of coal and air and water
        to purple heather-blossoms made from soil and sun and
        seed,
                        it isn't for us quarks to say.

It takes all kinds
        of black holes, so Thorne and Hawking say,
                to make a universe; it seems now that
there are some wandering still
                        left over from the early seconds of
        this present universe, so small their mass is only
                that of a granite mountain and their size
                        an average proton's—say
ten to the fourteenth power grams compressed into
        a speck of space that should, in classic theory, be
                unknowable,
except that like the Pentagon, these black holes leak,
        like Solomon's other seal they let
        out power that their *charm* won't hold,
                        their X-rays tunnel
out of the darkness like the songs of
        mockingbirds or sounds
                from bedroom windows: whether we
walk in moonlight or lie in private darkness,
        the shadows play us through,
the songs come down. That lullaby our Ponca aunt would sing,
        the one we always asked for when
                        sleep could not get to us past
the werewolves who howled
                inside the radio, she would sing to us
over and over, but she never told us, out there on
        the cool dark porch under the full moon,
what the Ponca words were saying: it was a song her blind
                great-aunt had made up after the Poncas
had been forced down from Nebraska onto
        the Oklahoma reservation, and she made it there
one night to sing her brothers when the whisky
                was almost drowning them: its words said,
                        Why are you afraid?
                        No one can go around death.

She tells her children lately now, Aunt Jewell, some of
    those real old things,
                        now that the time has come
to pass them on, and they are ready
    to make new places for what she
            would sing us in
    our moonlit darkness like
            a bronze and lively bird.

Making Money

Stamp a picture on some metal
that you've shaped thin and round,
and it's worth lots more.
Same way with planets:
draw your lines across one,
say you've divided it into
small pieces, and it's worth
a million times as much.
The closer you have drawn the lines,
the more each piece is worth.
A field you couldn't walk around in less
than half a day
won't pay its way
in fruit or cattle, honeybees or deer,
but cut it into single-acre lots
and you'll be rich.
Moons are worthless, but
look at the price of moon-rocks.
—This is all true, of course,
only if you can make a piece of paper
with certain lines drawn on it, curving
in shapes that we call names;
these marks combined
with arabesques that we call numbers
turn Paradise or Death Valley into
real estate, transform a tree
to money order, savages
into good citizens:
Blest paper credit, last and best supply,
That lends corruption lighter wings to fly,
as certain also of our own
poets have said.
Cities become the best machines
for generating capital, as it's called.
Look at them from the air at night,

the twinkling tentacles suckering
a wounded earth—
but in the daylight see the smudge
from which their twinkling comes,
then notice how the great lakes
and power stations in the desert lands
and in the mountains have become
their slaves, the clean air turned
to power and the sparkling lakes and rivers sending
pure heat and light into the heart
of great squared-off deserts of glass
and asphalt where the money's made.
What happens when the lines have all been drawn?
The cities die and rot from inside out,
the weeds come up through asphalt cracks,
blue chicory flowers grow across the sidewalks.
Bulldozers let them be: they're scraping clear
another Garden, toppling
old Trees of Life and Knowledge to plant
a Walmart where the shelves will hold
pulp mysteries and romances, exotic
apples and rattlesnake meat in plastic bags.

Transactions

Grand opening late April, say
the irises, we're selling
perfumes and colors for your life,
your only payment is the future.
We have to entertain
but only for a week or two
each year. Amazing value
you put on it, but who are we
to wonder why you like so much for us
to flaunt sex organs, purple or golden or
pure white, give us the well-tilled beds for orgies
with bees and butterflies and hummingbirds and when
that's finished let us disappear and carry on
underground like missionaries converting
the earth to Irisdom under the very
nose of humans.
Sometimes, of course, we're martyred—
cut down in purple prime and propped
in longstemmed crystal glinting
with rainbows while we're singing
Mi chiamano Mimi or maybe
Manibus o date lilia plena,
whatever coloratura
has been arranged for us,
the virgins sacrificed to keep the masters happy.
But hidden in our tuberous catacombs
we multiply ourselves and plan
the slow downfall of all those piles of brick
where humans sit with cut flowers on their tables thinking
they are the masters, we the slaves.

Earth and Diamonds

How far from truth to beauty, say
in diamonds?
Can we make either out of facts
put flatly, crunched together so their facets
crack light and spill
its rainbows over earth the way
plain carbon does when it is crushed into
a diamond, say?
A scientific fact was once
that stars made diamonds by their heavenly
"influence" acting deep within
the earth, mutating gunk
into bright gems;
but now it is a fact of science that earth
composes diamonds of itself—
and yet the earth itself was made
by superstars (another fact
of science, for the moment),
so that the house which stars once built
still crystallizes in the shape of stars, still
shines like them,
in language anyhow.
Of course
(you say) the earth, this common place, can't really shine.
But that's because we live too close to it:
the astronauts have seen
our muddy planet shine,
a blue star up in heaven.
That's what their eyes have seen:
their minds, of course, know very well it's not
a fact that's pure, it has
a flaw, depending on your point of view. It's air
that shines, and water mostly, earth
just holds these shining facts around
its heavy darkness.

So flights of angels, passing through our bodies,
may see a neutron shine
gemlike with facets, all the points of
inner structure netting
the radiant waves and fishing out
their rainbow messages of peace
from the God of Storms.
That, you'll say, is not
a fact—but if we just remove
the angels and insert
a physicist, you may allow
it is a fact though medaled
with metaphors and circumcised
by adjectives: yes,
our physicist might say,
it is a fact
that neutrons have a structure,
and perhaps that each is like
a crystal, certainly
neutrons are being probed by beams of
some other particles,
and in the spectrum which comes back to us
from deep inside these specks of space
are messages concerning Universal
Creation and Apocalypse.
Thus far we state pure facts, although
they are imperfect when they're packed into
the seedy figures of our speech,
and blossom only in the arabesques
of math, which has no fruitful symbols for
Creation and Apocalypse except
a change of signs.
—*FACT* meant *SOMETHING MADE*, in Roman mouths,
then English let it take the place of *TRUTH*.
Shakespeare was called, by Robert Greene,

"an absolute *FACTOTUM* in his own conceit."
He did it all,
that is, he *MADE* it all; instead of acting,
Shakespeare began to make the forms
for others' actions: yes, FACTOTUM,
that's the word.
People make diamonds now from coal, as easily
as they make perfume out
of oil, or pantyhose
from tar—
but diamonds we make
just as volcanoes did, with heat and pressure,
just as volcanoes were themselves
created by the moving
continents where the ocean's crust
dives under and the mountain-ship
floats over and begins to burn and thunder,
creating atmosphere, sunsets,
and diamonds in time.

And the male bowerbird creates his bower
to woo a mate, in fact the blue one chooses
only blue things to put in his,
he even mixes blue
paint and spreads it on his
bower's wall, using a piece of wood
or other brush to spread
the paint he's made from berries and
his way of seeing things.
But then, the fact is that
when once his mate is mated there
she leaves and builds her nest
and lays her eggs up in
some ordinary tree, and he just lets her go,

he takes no interest in the mortgage or the weather or the eggs, or in
those rising generations at their song,
he paints just what he sees, he makes
his gemlike house
of blue lights, keeps the species special and himself
fit to survive—and he's
a dinosaur, it seems, with warm blood, one
who put on feathers and survived: or so
facticians now assert as fact: the birds,
as Michael Castro says, are DYNA-SOARS!
If that is fact, we can no longer
believe that dinosaurs became extinct, just as we can
no longer hold that earth, not stars,
composes diamonds.
The trouble is, we keep exploding facts
into old myths, and then compressing myths
into new facts—
and so, in this dark kaleidoscope
of headlined findings, what once was
crystal clear becomes too nebulous
to be believed—
yet then becomes the evidence
that speaks of how our universe evolved,
as do the nebulae in space that once
were "clouds" and now are "ghosts"
of superstars that still broadcast the news
of brilliant bowers painted
upon the heavens long before
there was an earth
to sparkle bluely like a diamond in
the sky and make us wonder,
O twinkling little fact, just WHAT
you are: if true, how beautiful,
if beautiful, how true.

Amber and Lightning

Down the rough whale-road   I ride white-manes into
living-rooms, am wrapped   around word-wings,
dangle gold-lights   gleaming by love-fountains,
in shining time-windows   show the miniature
dragon-monsters flying   through millions of years—
sometimes as teeth   I sibilate through
the golden glory   of girls in mirrors,
freeing fireflies   to flash in darkness
electron, electron,   and lightning my name.

Snowflakes, Waterdrops, Time, Eternity and So On
For Bill and Carole

They tell me every snowflake
differs from every other one,
                    and yet,
so those who've looked insist,
they melt to waterdrops identical
each one with every other—
          this world I know's
a curious place, but who'd have thought those still
white mountaintops could capture difference,
those moving ocean waves identity,
while in between, the levity of clouds
keeps turning snow to rain or rain to snow,
and gravity's weird force has got us all
aspiring to disappear into
a singularity: who would believe
how those great powers wring
the music out of water over stones,
the rainbows out of waterfalls that silver
a mountainside with streams like veins
in a maple leaf keeping delighted eyes
from April sun—
green leaf trembling up here from loam
which over there has been called forth
as columbine and ponderosa: Listen, how all
those Trickster seeds and Coyote clouds, those
big bangers say
let there be light,
and darkness fountains dawn like
a trumpet's golden one-way where breath
goes in, Mozart comes out.
So let the two
be one,
snowflake and waterdrop,
tomorrow and today,
maple tree and columbine,

                    let us drink,
in fact, to weddings, bottoms up
with this sparkling champagne that is water
with a difference, its snowy bubbles briefly
dancing upon our tongues and rioting
within our veins and aching, it may be,
within our heads,
but not with grief,
not with regret, only
the knowledge that we'll have
our differences, and may
we thank God for them every day.

Unzipping Angels

[Words are the Daughters of Men; Things are the Sons of Heaven.—
Samuel Johnson]
[When Adam asked what angels did, Raphael,
          . . . with a smile that glowed
Celestial rosy red, love's proper hue,
Answered: " Let it suffice thee that thou know'st
Us happy, and without love no happiness.
Easier than air with air, if spirits embrace,
Total they mix, union of pure with pure
Desiring; nor restrained conveyance need
As flesh to mix with flesh, or soul with soul."
                                    —*Paradise Lost* 8.618-29]

Angels don't look
through human eyes—
they see
us all at once, voyaging timeless and
capsuled in dream they taste
on the baby's lips the
dying President's blood;
their Mœbius strip of synæsthesia pulls
up sticky from the tomb of THERE
the phoenix-nest of HERE, and from their gummy
fragments resubstantiates those glorious
sunsets of 1883 into the surf-
fringed mountain peak of Krakatoa even
while watching this universe start up and
end like a beating heart. And yet—
and yet—
CAN they know people,
know TIME as we do, bear
our mortal awareness,
our carnal knowledge? When,
for instance, the Sons of God looked
upon the Daughters of Men
and found them fair,
how far into such deep

blue eyes could they
descend? Was it
at first like
leaving behind the curving arms
of a galaxy for
one blue star expanding heartwise into
the white-marbled swirl of weather,
then down, down into bronze, into
bluegreen ocean and desert, only
to land in a
parking lot, empty, with
shopping carts
whinging in gusts of wind
on a closed Sabbath?
Or was it deep-illusioning,
like moth-wings touching
her eyelids, the irised curtains open and
they taste
their mintlike minds,
papaya senses,
feelings like milk and
honey, hot wholewheat
caritas? What being burns through both as
star-myriads enter turning
the skin of space away in
flares of shining
ungraves, her hips
rising weightless poised as
in 3-D sliding above
white crinkle of Everest,
deep
blue
shimmer of being in
time growing small,
blue point in darkness dropping

on a dark cry into
unself where they move,
on starry rapids riding down
deep swells like dolphins through
white foam and all
of time a graceful curving as
of dolphins in the deep
surges of dancing gently upon
the pointless point of
         their heavenly joy.

Christmas Shopping

You know, there's a Venture
parking lot which offers,
maybe three times a year,
free sunsets of the highest
order—only one
per person admittedly, but well
worth driving up there for. Stella and
I were up there, this December,
Christmas shopping, and one became
available with evening
star thrown in—
what happened was this western
horizon all spilled over with a
kind of gold
translucence shining among
shadowy rooftops and the asphalt
streets falling away beneath
where we pulled out of this
Venture—
Well, *shining among*—not really,
you know, what
I want your mind's
eye to see. How to say it?
Look,
off a high asphalt blackness over into this
dim gold brilliance with dark
houses and rooftops, TV aerials, electric wires
with squirrels hotfooting above the honk and
car-dazzle—
        ah, SHADOWTAIL! that's what
the word *squirrel* once meant!—no, still
not getting this across. See, we were driving
out of this parking lot,
and when we'd gone in it was just a
late afternoon, and we hadn't bought a thing in

there, we came out empty and kind of,
you know, money just couldn't find its
objective correlative—the things we looked at,
the money, they wouldn't fall in love. People
wouldn't maybe WANT them.
What happens when
even the credit cards have failed you and
that whole huge building full of wantables
which everybody's furiously buying for their loved
ones doesn't have what you want, and so we
came back out . . . but where blue sky and plain
daylight had been
was semi-twilight that
as well as getting
darker was filling up with light, not dazzling
but brilliant—the cars did have their
lights on, too bright to look into, and red tail-lights
were—you could practically
taste them, but they fitted,
they hung upon the cheeks of twilight
like rubies from an Ethiop's ear,
to pluck the Swan
of Avon's phrase. You know what
I mean, LUMINOUS rhymes
with NUMINOUS—nothing was ordinary, it seemed
we'd floated up into the sunset air all
filled with gold and dark shining, like
being in a cathedral with the moon and not a
Venture parking lot,
the light was different so
the earth was too. Well, so
that was the first I'd noticed this Venture was up on
a hill and we were looking out across
the city to the south,
its houses

[84]

stood in this purity, this
undersea kind of tranquil
brilliance without glitter,
but stars just coming out, the first
one huge and bright over
the sunset where it turned to night sky and
blue like where deep water
becomes pure blackness, not a wall but
a medium you could move into,
and this is what I'm getting at, the houses were
as well placed as that evening star, they didn't
need to shine, the air
was doing all that for them—
AHA! so how much is it? where's the
wrapping paper? Will you take
the Master Card or Visa, or the gold
American Express? Bleep, bleep-bleep,
bleep! O NO! The big computer in the sky
takes words, and only if I haven't spent
too many on unwanted things. Now I've reached
the limit for this gift. I hope what's wrapped in this
is Christmas Eve with sunset
in St. Louis,
                    but
you may find only words. If you're lucky though,
your house and car's included, not to
mention that whole VENTURE, full of THINGS IN THEMSELVES
watched by a squirrel sitting with tail curved like
a winter-warming question, white
belly shining in the last of
twilight on the heavy electric line that
crosses Page Avenue
                    and this page now.

Given
—*for the children*

this world to grow into, I know
they'll repossess it shortly, along with
what's left of me—yet, rumpled
into this little pocket
of time, I wish
there were a little more of me to sing
the mortgage payments—how it really
dawns on me this morning as
the light has brimmed and spills all rosy into
the east with robins paying
their rent in song and with the downy
woodpecker's telephone-pole tattoo explaining
the nod of daffodils and endless
pinoaks, maples, ash and sycamore and locusts,
sweetgum dogwood and redbud bowing into the April
windstream over
us blind and flightless creatures blundering
noisy and slow as brachiosaurs, squeaking and rumbling
like humpback whales beneath quick birds where they
are singing that the springing wealth of new
leaves and light and flowers has made it
practical to consummate the mystery of
nesting, if
within earshot the right females would return
the secret signs that they will partner them.
We see, we *learn*
to see and hear and feel, the way
those leaves come out of buds all tight
with liquid virtue rising from earth-blind roots
into bright air to fan
their soft translucent green as
they ask the light into their bowers
of sugars, starches, lignins, as we see
in green and hear in song how light
becomes a tree and holds

the singers in its branches where curving
and blue as sky small eggs will open
and blind reptilian robins fledge and find how
to sing the light back into dawn,
their arias and duets soaring above starsongs
of tree-frogs in the summer dark, just as
into translucent salmon sunrise the stars
dissolve, white clouds set sail across
the blue dazzle above us walking on
our stony earth where clopping
and grating we look up into
those heavens of green and blue and white where the trees
without moving are given the earth and
the sun and the stars, and those who have wings now
are singing and those who have climbed
from sea to earth and air and live now on dew and the tree's
plenty are singing where the moon brings back
a softer light from the sun, where the stars bring us the great
glittering darkness that has no end.

Liquid Crystal Thoughts

Looking through windshields at sixty-three
years in a seventy-year zone,
I see how this liquid crystal—invented by
volcanoes often, Egyptians somewhat later—
helps us gaze into our age; I see
these beads were WORTH Manhattan maybe, see
glass pluck and cobbler
dark-shining galaxies, brush time away to make
some quasar from a billion years ago
shine freshly in the barrel of our scopes—
see how it gives
champagne a shape with freedom to
send up its bubbles into hearts yet
how acidly the Hasselblads
etch time into our faces, how glass
papparazzis Amoeba's private lives,
makes Japanese characters Shinto through
its tiny glintzy tubes
into St. Louis,
puts Christmas onto rootless trees,
holds flowers (compare the way earth holds them by the roots)
in water, dying, lets us say
have a glass, not have a plastic—
corrects our visions,
fends off passes,
glass-harmonicates,
swings from the ceilings letting candles
make recreation out of procreation and calls it
chandeliers—is liquid
crystal reality, amazing
the physicists one more time. And sharp;
the insulating stuff that kept us warm,
glass wool they called it, would cut
us to pieces everywhere inside
and so is banned. Look at a gob

twirled on its rod, glowing golden
honey for Hephaestos, and then
the human breath goes in,
the vase will hold
all Venice, Titian's colors and the sea.

Sea-changes, Easter 1990
Phi Beta Kappa Poem, University of Tulsa, 4 May 1990
(For Don and Mary Frances Hayden)

Where the electron gun targets the screen
between the past and us, we push
the buttons that will resurrect
THE LIVING WORLD within our living room, so we
can watch dolphin and diver try
to comprehend each other's mind,
The mind, that ocean where each kind
Does straight its own resemblance find;
Yet it creates, transcending these,
Far other worlds, and other seas:

we sink down where
the pale blue quivers as a dolphin swims
out of her dark shadows into
our hearts and minds. I think she hears, mostly,
a plume of silver bubbles rising from
this clumsy alien and the buzzing box he holds,
some glass-eyed thing that never, so far
as the dolphin knows, looks back at her—

yet here, from deep behind its glass
in this *dark forward and abysm of time,*
we sit looking into that dolphin's eyes and wonder
what goes on deep within her where
a consciousness of self and us might be. And words
come bubbling from our television, spoken
months later and thousands of miles away from where
diver and dolphin face each other, saying:
"We tried to speak with dolphins—knowing
they have a kind of language, we were hoping
to send a message."

—Now the diver has carried down into
the dreaming turquoise of

the dolphin's parlor ordinary jars:
they might be fruit-juice jars but in this medium they
morph into sun-seines, crystal star-traps—and now
the diver takes his air-tube from his mouth,
inverts a jar and jams the tube up into
its mouth so silver bubbles fill
it with brilliant air and then
he does it to other jars, two, THREE of them,
and see, he's got a little rod to tap them with—
he's tapping, and we hear each jar
respond with different tone, he makes almost
a tune—it is enchanting, and look—from shadows there
offstage the dolphin eases toward the jars, she noses
up past them, eying
the diver and his jars, she clearly
listens, and looks, and wonders maybe ... ah no,
she turns, and her tail waves like a conductor damping down
to pianissimo, she swims away into
the darkness, saying with her whole body:
They'll NEVER speak: they have no music!

Disappointed, the diver
descends now to the white fine sand
of the seabottom and glances towards the anchor-chain
of the boat he's dived from, trailing there. He reaches down,
he picks it up, he looks: we see
the chainlinks glitter, hear the clinks
and scrapes, we see the anchor's flukes
unfold, as he lifts it, in his weightless dreamlit
heaven of Zuni silversmiths where he has set
the turquoise tingling with his silver anchorchain—
and SWIFTLY NOW from where
the blue turns black, a shape comes hurtling, but
she turns and slows, she passes over the jangling
silver chain, she looks,

listens, poises
quite upside down and drifts, beak slightly open, listens to
those tinny squeaks, clinks, scrapings, clanks: her eyes
lost in ecstatic hearing, her head as close
to the chain as she can get, saying:
At last, a Tristan for my Isolde. how could they ever
encrypt this miracle of music in such links of light, who
could ever have composed it and was he the greatest
lover of all the dolphins in the world?

—Well, OF COURSE!
We always knew the messages we sent
with Voyager would get across, though what
we didn't know was what those messages might mean:
the Navajo Night Chant, maybe THAT would heal
the wars out there. or would it take
the sound of crickets, or the clink
of chains in medieval dungeons. Perhaps the rasping
of dull razorblades across
a three-day stubble, or the screek
of chalk on blackboards, THAT
will be Beethoven—
our long-dead Star rising to shine within
their WAVE OF FAME. *Humans,*
they'll maybe say,
they can't be ALL bad, if they can sing like that!

But there's a DOWN side, though—
could be, Beethoven's Ninth
and its great Ode to Joy
will translate as a declaration of merciless
war upon the beings of the first
palm-fringed star where Voyager
has washed up with our brittle jetsam.
—What DID the Aztecs hear, when the white sails

of Cortez rose from a turquoise sea?
Five hundred years ago, we've heard,
five hundred years ago Columbus came:
what messages our people then exchanged, what chains
of promises we heard. AND buffaloes, passenger pigeons,
Pequods and Mohicans heard: "we" sent "them"
tomatoes and syphilis, "they" gave "us"
the Civil Wars of aliens.
So now we peer
into the eyes of natives trapped in the ruined walls
of Dresden, Hue, Beirut, El Salvador—
EL SALVADOR!
paralyzed children staring
into the Pulitzer Prizes of our televising selves,
on Easter Sunday like flying fish we skim
the rainbow waves of
a Religious Channel, purpled by the death
and resurrection of that Savior
whom Michaelangelo sculpted for his Pope—
breakfasting at home,
we look down from within the dome
of St. Peter's there in Rome:
what music's there, what anchorchains
of hope, what alien sounds
we roll away the tombstones from, what alien eyes
we look into and try to comprehend.

Law and Order

Discovery of the New World

The creatures that we met this morning
marveled at our green skins
                    and scarlet eyes.
They lack antennae
        and can't be made to grasp
                    your proclamation that they are
our lawful food and prey and slaves,
        nor can they seem to learn
                    their body-space is needed to materialize
our oxygen-absorbers—which they
        conceive are breathing and thinking
                    creatures whom they implore
at first as angels, then as devils,
        when they are being snuffed out
        by an absorber swelling
                    into their space.
Their history bled from one this morning,
        while we were tasting its brain,
which we assembled into quite an interesting
        set of legends—
                    that's all it came to, though
the colors were quite lovely before we
        poured them into our time;
                    the blue shift bleached away
meaningless circumstances, and they would not fit
        any of our truth-matrices—
                    there was, however,
a curious visual echo in their legends
        of our own coming to their earth:
        a certain General Sherman said
        about one group of them precisely what
        we have been telling you about these creatures:
        it is our destiny to asterize this planet,
                    and they will NOT
                    be asterized, so they

must be wiped out.
We NEED their space and nitrogen,
which they do not know how to *use*,
nor will they breathe ammonia, as we do—
yet they will not give up their "air" unforced,
so it is clear,
whatever our "agreements" made this morning,
we'll have to kill them all:
the more we cook this orbit,
the fewer next time round.
We've finished lazing all their crops and stores,
we've killed their meat-slaves, now
they'll have to come into our pens,
and we can use them for our final studies
of how our heart attacks and cancers spread among them, since
they seem not immune to these.
—If we didn't have this mission, it might be sad
to watch these helpless creatures die chanting
their sacred psalms and bills of rights; but never fear,
the riches of this globe are ours,
and worth whatever pains others may have to feel.
We'll soon have it cleared
completely, as it now is at the poles, and then
we will be safe, and rich, and happy here, forever.

November in Washington, D.C.

The guards are *friendly* when you walk
at night up toward the Capitol, standing floodlit
white and shining above
its Roman pillars—
"Good evening, where are you folks from?"
"Ah, St. Louis—we live there."
"Faan-TAS-tic!"—
but there's an interruption,
a siren and a flashing cop-car swirling up
through the parking lot behind two lost
cars filled with tourist families
—or maybe terrorists?
But then the cars stop, the cop's
lights stop flashing, there's a *friendly*
palaver and they swing around and drive
out down the street,
and the young *friendly* guard, mustached,
in black gloves and overcoat, who has
been watching us and them, pounds
his gloved hands and says again "FanTASTic!" in a way
that means he's checked us out, so we
walk on, around the Capitol
and down dark steps and sidewalk to the
Reflecting Pool—it must be
several acres of still and
shimmering dark alive
with streetlights, brilliant green
and red of traffic signals, tail-lights's Red Glare—
and then, from its other side, we see
the white unreal dome of the Capitol in it,
pointing down, down, at a star glittering deep
in the pool below it, a large bright
star—Venus, we think. At the moment,
this most powerful building in the world's
asleep in Xanadu

(*a little water clears it of its deeds*),
a Pleasure Dome where people
—Chinese? Japanese? are setting up their cameras now
to capture Pool and Capitol in one silver shot.
We could walk further, down the Mall,
and past the National Gallery where
they've captured Veronese's paintings for a time—
or by the Space Museum, where Astronauts
are dummies in their capsules, and
sleek missile-launchers stand like Michaels *waiting*
to stop Time for us
(*they also served*)—
or past the Smithsonian, where (I'm told)
the symbols of our Osage people wait, that let
us come down from the stars to form
a nation, here.
Instead, the night being damp, we turn
and walk on back along East Capitol, past
some trash receptacles on whose dull orange, painted
in yellow profile, is a *Redskin*—
RE-located from the *Buffalo Nickel*—
and now *PRESIDENT* over
the old news of this 1988 election, as we
walk eastward, into the full
and orange moon.

History into Words

(In 1645-6, while besieged in Oxford by Cromwellian forces, King
Charles I used Christ Church College and its cathedral church as
headquarters.)

        I think of John Roberts, historian and
                Warden of Merton College, writing
        a history of Europe, walking
                in late September maybe,
        down the broad
                caramel-gravelled walk between
Christ Church Cathedral and Merton Meadows. The sky
        is blue this afternoon with high
cloud-wisps so bright they make
                him squint glancing up. When he looks through
                        the locked and steel-barred gate
                past the wall's grey stones
        into the flowers at its base and edging
                        the gate's both sides, he looks
                over a shaven lawn and at the smallest
        cathedral in England. Crimson and
                        creamy roses frame the spire, a
        blue sky edges its shadowed walls. Then between
                the gate's black bars a breath
        of breeze brings scintillation and his eyes
                        now focus on a billowing web,
                its small and gently flexing circles holding
        this butterfly of time whose wings mother
                our hurricanes, this delicate
                        fossil jihad,
        this small cathedral in its silken orb.

Another Sunday Morning

What I walked down to the highway for,
                     through the summer dawn,
                          was the Sunday funnies,
               or so I thought—
                     but what I remember reading there
               in the shadowless light
                          among meadowlarks singing
          was tracks in the deep warm dust
                     of the lane, where it parted
               with its beige dryness the meadow's dew—
     the sleek trail where a snake had crossed
          and slid into tall grass;
                     the stippled parallels
     with marks between them where
                          a black blister-beetle had dragged
               its bulbous belly across
          in search of weeds more green;
                          the labyrinth of lacelike
     dimples left by a speed-freak
                     tiger-beetle's sprints that ended
                     where it took wing
          with a little blur of dust-grains;
                     and stepping through the beetle-trails,
     the wedge-heels and sharp-clawed hands of a skunk-track
               crossing unhurried and walking
                    along the ditch to find
                    an easy place for climbing;
not far past that,
          a line of cat-prints running
                               straight down the lane and ending
          with deep marks where it leaped
                          across the ditch to the meadow
               for birds asleep or wandering baby rabbits:
and freshly placed this morning,
                          the slender runes

                              of bob-whites running, scuffles
                  of dustbaths taken—
                      and there ahead
        crouched low at the lane-edge
                          under purple pokeweed-berries
                  four quail had seen me,
                  and when I walked slowly
                  on toward them, instead
                      of flying they ran
        with a fluid scuttling
                              on down the lane and stopped frozen
                                  till I came too close
                  —then quietly when
                  I expected an explosion
          of wings they took off low and whispering
              and sailed, rocking and tilting
                              out over the meadow's tall bluestem,
              dropped down and were gone until
        I heard them whistling, down by the little pond,
                  and whistled back so sharply
              that when I got back to the house
                  they still were answering
                  and one flew into the elm
                  and whistled from its shadows
                              up over the porch where I sat
        reading the funnies while the kittens
                      played with the headlines
                              till when the first gold sunlight
                  tipped the elm's leaves he flew
        back out to the meadow and sank
                          down into sun-brilliant dew
                      on curving wings,
              and my brothers and sisters waked
                          by the whistling came pouring out
          onto the porch and claimed their share

of the Sunday funnies—
and I went on to read
the headlines of World War Two,
with maps of the struggling armies leaving
tank-tracks over the dunes of Libya
and the navies churning their wakes
of phosphorescence in the Coral Sea
where the ships went down on fire
and the waves bobbed and flamed
with the maimed survivors, screaming
in Japanese or English until
their gasoline-blistered heads
sank down to the tiger sharks
and the war was lost or won
for children sitting in sunlight,
believing their cause was just
and knowing it would prevail,
as the dew vanished away.

Parading with the Veterans of **Foreign** Wars

Apache, Omaha, Osage, Choctaw, Comanche, Cherokee, Oglala,
    Micmac:
our place was ninety-fifth,
and when we got there with our ribbon shirts
and drum and singers on the trailer,
women in shawls and traditional dresses,
we looked into the muzzle of
an Army howitzer in front of us.
"Hey, Cliff," I said,
haven't seen guns that big
since we were in Wounded Knee."
Cliff carried the new American flag
donated by another post; Cliff prays
in Omaha for us, being chairman
of our Powwow Committee, and his prayers
keep us together, helped
by hard work from the rest of course.
"They'll move that one-oh-five ahead," Cliff said.
They did, but then the cavalry arrived.
No kidding, there was this troop outfitted
with Civil War style uniforms and carbines,
on horseback, metal clopping on
the asphalt street, and there
on jackets were the insignia:
the Seventh Cavalry, George Custer's bunch.
"Cliff," Walt said, "they think you're Sitting Bull."
"Just watch out where you're stepping, Walt,"
Cliff said, "Those pooper-scoopers
will not be working when the parade begins."
"Us women walking behind the trailer
will have to step around it all
so much, they'll think we're dancing,"
was all that Sherry said.
We followed
the yellow line, and here and there

some fake war-whoops came out to us
from sidewalk faces, but applause
moved with us when the singers started,
and we got our banners seen announcing
this year's Pow-Wow in June,
free to the public in Jefferson Barracks Park—
where the Dragoons were quartered for the Indian Wars.
When we had passed the Judging Stand
and pulled off to the little park all
green and daffodilly under the misting rain,
we put the shawls and clothing in the cars
and went back to the Indian Center, while
Cliff and George Coon went out and got
some chicken from the Colonel
that tasted great, given the temporary
absence of buffalo here in the
Gateway to the West, St. Louis.

Coming of Age in the County Jail

—I see they worked you over. What you in for?
—Oh, I took this kiddie-car out of a guy's back yard, Friday
    midnight.
—What in the world gave you the idea for that?
—Celebrate my birthday. Me and George decided we'd haul it up
    on top the Mound, ride down on that kiddie-car,
    see if we could finish off the wine on the way down.
—That how you got the black eye and stitches, no doubt.
—Not hardly. Turned out the guy whose yard we took it from
    was a city cop, he saw us put it in our car
    and start off down the Mound Road.
—Where'd they catch up with you?
—We got out near the Mound and here came three patrol cars
    with sirens
    and red lights flashing, blocked off the road,
    big mob of police jumped out with guns.
—Well, what did you say to them?
—Mostly we said ow and that's enough. I made the mistake
    of hitting back at a couple. After they got me down
    in back of the car with handcuffs on behind my back,
    they beat me on the shoulderblades with blackjacks.
    This cut in my eyebrow's from a pistol though.
—Yeah, looks like it. What are you charged with now?
—There's a pretty good list of things they mentioned. Felony,
    for taking the kiddie-car, which the officer valued
    at over fifty dollars; then there's assaulting an officer,
    resisting arrest, driving with open bottle,
    disturbing the peace, so on and so on.
—Well, nobody wants to have his kid's things stolen, especially
    police.
    but maybe that lawyer can get the charge reduced
    to misdemeanor, once things cool down a little.
    They told me fifteen minutes was all I had,
    I'll start back now. Well, don't wander off.

—No, I kind of think they'll let me stay till the hearing. Besides, the service here's just great, and gourmet cooking. Well, here's the man. Thanks for dropping in.

Free White and Fifteen

When the bullet hit, the horse keeled over dead.
The little kids cried that had ridden on him all week,
But hell, he was bought to feed the dogs, not ride on,
Old broken-down plowhorse, gentle or not.
We hitched the tractor, hooked him onto the platform;
John skinned the head, chest mine, Buster the belly,
By then tight-bloated: Buster slit through
And bloof! a spray-spout of bloody piss shot upward
Drenching Buster on face and body and hair.
Well, I broke out laughing and Buster went nuts,
He waved his skinning knife and came after me.
I swung and knocked him back on the flayed ribs,
Knocked down the middle knuckle on my right hand.
He raised up glaring at me for half a second,
Then flopped back flat, eyes rolled up and closed,
Just spread his arms like sleeping and lay dead still.
The smell of piss and blood came back with hand-hurt,
The rush of greyhounds jumping and barking, racing
Each other up and down the kennel fences.
"If you damn fools have had your fun," Johnny said,
"Let's get this horse cut up." I hopped around
On the bloody slippery platform, got my knuckle back,
Then Buster sat up. He didn't recall getting drenched
But after a rest he felt like working again.
We salted, folded the hide, flopped it into a barrel.
We gutted, quartered, carved meat like cherry Jello
In chunks, tossed slivers to favorite dogs.
—That night, Buster and I were going to a movie.
We never got there. His head still hurt. Instead,
We thumbed in to his house, where I'd never been.
His folks weren't there. Hadn't seen them lately, he said,
But they'd turn up and want some of his money
Before too long. He'd drink it up first, enjoy it.
One of these days the old man would wake up
With a butcher knife in his back if he kept taking money.

One room was Buster's. Linoleum cracked, floor warping,
Bare bulb—all over the floor and on the bed
Comic books, pulp Westerns, detective magazines
Open with torn pages, the bed unmade.
He could spend whole days just reading things.
Sometimes all Sunday he wouldn't go out of his room,
Just lay there reading. He could write better
Than some of these guys, was going to rent a typewriter.
—We finally walked downtown and looked around.
Plenty of girls, but hell, they wanted cars
And guys with money. Us, we carried the stink
Of twelve hours' work at lowpaid country jobs,
Nowhere to take them, couldn't even hand out a line
Worth giggling over. Finally I had to get home.
Buster stood waiting while I tried to thumb.
Waited so long we walked across the street
To Old Man Brokeback's stand and snatched two pears—
Had to run like hell. A car finally stopped.
We'd be at work next morning, cleaning kennels.

Firewater

Sometimes I think how alcohol's
a marvelous solvent, can remove
red people from a continent,
turn bronze to guilt. What was DuPont's
old motto—Better things
for better living
through chemistry? You take
potatoes from Peru,
barley from Palestine, maize
from Mexico, sugar cane
from Indo-China—
put in some wild yeast from the air,
ferment it and *voila!* you've now
got Vodka for the Volga, beer
for the Brits, Bourbon for
Balboa's kids, Joy-juice for
the Kickapoos.
Pour this into an Inner City and create
your Designated Criminal Class purely
to blame for everything,
or rub it on the Reservations and you'll see
each fetus wizen up inside
its fertile womb.
Yet drip it into the veins
of Congress or a Corporation, just watch
those Mountain Men outrassle steers,
gulping their liquid god go wildly
enthusiastic so they can
write laws in stone with one hand while
joysticking lovers with the other,
sacking Montana and out-dunking Jordan,
out-leveraging—who was it,
Archimedes, popped the world's blue eyeball
into a Swiss snowbank. See, ghettoites,
how sociable our masters are,

these Bacchanalians, never alcoholic,
immune in suburbs where bad sex has died
and gone to heaven, no AIDS, no illegitimate
children, all the schools
have classic curricula and every personal fetus
will be delivered right on time,
uncorked like Chateauneuf du Pape, unscrewed
like Southern Comfort to gurgle on
its snowy tablecloth, caress with rosy fingers
its parents' egos and become
a tax loophole. Classic,
ah Classic these Metamorphoses of Dionysos—
but please, be careful how you tell of them,
remember Ovid shivering on
the Black Sea shores, wondering how to get back in
to one of the Roman villas once again.

A Response to Terrorists

It seems you can't
stay bottom dog too long
before some other bunch
outbottoms you. Frankly,
speaking as Indian I admit
it's easier to be noble and smile
while vanishing, just as for Martin Luther King
in prison it was easier than
for Andrew Young as Ambassador—
and last year's victims of the Holocaust
are next year's seekers of Lebensraum
in Lebanon: the Palestinians are
the ones in concentration camps these days.
Isn't there some way we might
get out from under without finding ourselves
on top and smothering others?
Oh sure,
it seems unlikely that the Acoma
will buy out Kerr-McGee
and claim New Mexico as theirs, or that
the Iroquois will get the Adirondacks back
and run a leveraged buyout of
the Chase Manhattan, Rupert Murdoch, and the Ivy League.
But if they did,
would they be citizens at last of the Great
Imperial Order, rather than our kind of
small endangered cultures where the sense
of needing every one of us,
of being the tip of growth, the quick
of living earth,
is borne in on us by our smallness,
our clear fragility?
It's feeling powerful and yet
afraid that fuels killing,
        it's knowing we are weak and brave

that lets us want to live
            and let live. The terrorists—Reader,
fill in the names of heads of government as you
read this: their names were once
(perhaps before your time)
Reagan, Gorbachev, Shamir, Khaddafy,
Thatcher, D'Aubuisson, among the rest—
                    would they knife THEIR mothers,
shatter a GRANDchild's head against a wall or even
terrify kittens with a stun grenade?
                        They murder with
their tongues, send surrogates
        to knife, garotte, beat, poison, torture—who
            could count the ways? This
is a tiger: fire off a missile and the monster will
        retreat and show respect. The kitten's
flayed, comes out a foot with self-inflicted
        bullet-hole, flapping like
a tongue. Forked tongue. Ah, look
how they leave the Summit, now,
climb in their stretch limos and drive away,
        not skidding on
    the grandchild's brains.

Hamlet and Fortinbras Exchange Pleasantries

(An excerpt from HAMLET: THE REAL STORY. *The Private Journal of Horatio, friend to Hamlet, Prince of Denmark*, as discovered by an enterprising biographer of the Danish royal family in Vatican Library MS. Petrificus 666, fols. 17v–18r.)

HAMLET: All right, you've taken Denmark and they're cheering,
The poison's got me, put away your knife—
But let me tell you what you'd better know
Unless you want it to be used against you.
Your mother never told you we were brothers?
Look in the archives, once you've taken over—
The ones dear Uncle Claudius used for blackmail.
They thought I sneaked back there to meet Ophelia,
And so I did, and I made sure they heard us,
But "Carnal Knowledge" and "Affairs of State"
Are filed together, at our royal level.
Something Polonius dropped gave them away.
Why do you think "your" father hated mine?
Revenge is very nice. Now I've had mine,
You're having yours, you think—but what you need's
The truth, which makes revenge impossible
For any son of a bitch like you or me.
Whatever you may touch, you'll make more slimy,
Not clean it up. But you can trample through it—
This royal sty won't bother studs like you,
You can ignore the hissing chattering mouths
Of skeletons in closets; you'd hardly mind
A nightmare kiss from someone you'd deflowered
Who drowned herself. Power that's fried my brain
Is just a twinkle in your baby blues.

FORTINBRAS: Your ignorance, not my power, makes me laugh.
We're cousins, Hamlet. Claudius was your dad,
Ophelia your half-sister, but Laertes
Was my half-brother. Go ahead and laugh—

You've earned it, cousin, being such a fool.
As for Horatio here, your paramour,
You may not want to know whose son he is—
But just between us, coz, I'll tell you, since
Your mouth's forever sealed: Polonius was
The doddering source of all his "Milord" ways.
Now, never fear, Norway will take good care
Of Denmark when you're dead and rotten, which
I see will be quite soon. Goodbye, dear cousin—
Your fathers are avenged, and so are mine.

The Biograbbers
(reading a new bio-chapter on Robert Frost in "The American Scholar")

A mobile home is not the smartest place
to view tornadoes from,
particularly when
one's coming right up the pipe
to get you, as it was
when my brother Addison had stripped down
to his jockstrap there in Lawrence, Kansas—
he'd finished teaching math that day
at Haskell and was going to put on sweats
and go out jogging,
but suddenly found himself
and mobile home like a tumbleweed bounding
across the asphalt and it dumped him out
the window after a block or so—
he picked himself up
and was barely bruised though considerably
surprised, among
a lot of trash which had
been treasured by whoever lived
in all those places where hail and wind and lightning entered
and broke and scattered all that
was in those kitchens, beds, desks, cabinets, lives.
And so a colleague asked him
the next day, after the sorting out
of deaths and lives and photographs, after
the looting and the picking up of things
had gone on for that while,
"Well, Addison, what were you thinking about
when you were getting tumbled across that lot?"
"I was just wondering," my brother said,
"if I was wearing any clothes."
Ah well, if you're lucky, Junior,
and never run for President
or wake up and find yourself like Byron or Frost
a famous man, you needn't worry how

the winds of history blow.
They'll put us in decent clothes, they may
even not photograph us dead and naked,
at least so far even newspapers
have not been quite that shameless,
and television, though it likes to find some victim
and family to spread for money, hasn't
so far as I know camcord-snouted down
so deep in Dante's hell as that; they let
anonymous remnants of a storm alone,
they pay for titillating closeups only
of famous people. It's true they've added
to death new terrors, but still
they'll have to recognize us first, only then
would fame make it worth while—
because good news is no news—
to rip us up, flay us then pose smugly next to autoptotic slides
of auto-immune lesions in our minds, the DNA
of diseased sexuality, aspirins still drawing blood
in capitalistic bellies, a raised eyebrow revealing
an Oedipus or a Sphincter complex above our dead eyes still GAZING
monstrously upon whatever woman walks within their ken
or criminally scrying how
such biograbbers paw through these crumpled remains or kick
them drenched and scattered across the vacant lot
of history where we lived.

Support your Local Police Dog

The night before Uncle Carter got shot dead
Trying to hijack a load of bootleg whiskey,
He dressed fit to kill, put on his lilac hairoil
And leaned down to the mirror in our living room
To comb the hair back over his bald spot, humming,
"Corinne, Corin-ne, where have you been so long?"
I don't know if "Corinne" tipped the other bunch off,
But I hope he made it with her before they killed him.
I bet if there was any, he was getting his—
Jesus, I never saw him standing still
Or lying down, till they led me past his coffin.
He should've been born a lord in Boswell's time,
Though he'd most likely been laid up with gout
Before he was forty, had that uric drive.
More drive than brains, though. Hell, out on parole
For robbing a bank, his hip not very long healed
Where the cop in ambush shot him trying to surrender,
Had no more sense than go after those bottled-in-bonders
From Kansas City. You *know* they'd be in cahoots
With local crooks and laws. We couldn't see why
A man with his brains ever got talked into trying.
My Uncle Dwain said must've been a put-up job,
He knew too much, the gang'd had him bumped off.
Well, the last time I was home for a visit,
Our Oklahoma voters had just made whiskey legal,
But I'd been living with earnest city people
That keep *discovering* crime and poverty
Like tin cans tied to their suburbs' purebred tails
Till they run frothing, yapping for law and order,
So turning from U.S. Sixty off to our house,
I thought of the big police dog Carter brought home
His last time there, and kennelled by the chickenhouse.
Nobody was going to steal our stock, by God.
—Later, the damn dog got to killing turkeys
On a neighbor's place; we had to let it be shot.

The gilt mirror Carter peered at his bald spot in
Had been demoted, now hung dim in the bathroom.
I patted the Old Spice lather on and shaved
As suavely as he had combed, and smelled as good—
He never lived to grow white whiskers like mine.
I knew the smartest crooks don't ever need guns,
And I would never walk out into the night
To get myself shot down, the way he did.
I've got more brains. But while he lived, I admit,
He was my favorite uncle: guts, charm, and drive.
He would have made a perfect suburban mayor—
Or later, manager for some liquor chain.

Criminals as Creators of Capital

I don't know how we'd ever get along
        without our criminals. Think how many
jobs it takes to support one criminal.
        First off, the jails. The architects it takes
to plan them, then the bricklayers,
        all the steel rod makers to reinforce
                the concrete and to bar the windows.
The lawyers—my God there alone is half
the budget of a Roman emperor:
        lawyers to prove them guilty, lawyers to show
they're innocent, lawyers to fiddle
        their taxes for them, lawyers to help
appeal the appeals of appeals—
        and then the inventors, those who make the locks
and those who find the keys.
        Bomb-makers, gun-makers, pawnshops and right-wing
gun-nuts and their media-shills, handcuff makers, a whole
        damned set
of manufacturers—
                        of poison gas pellets, hypodermics,
electric chairs, gallows ropes and prison chaplains
        (I wonder if the guy that invented
                the hangman's knot obtained a patent for it?).
Then, of course, all the police, the FBI,
        the SEC, SWAT teams, the whole damned airport
security bunch and the Homeland Security Inquisitors,
        the Secret Service, their bulletproofs and cellphones,
their transportation, housing, poison-tasters, snipers,
        that whole damned pile of special gear, gumshoes and all.
The teargas makers, shoulder holster,
        stun-gun, Taser, and billyclub makers. Dome lights for
                police cars, the gasoline for all
        that driving round and round the block. Electric lights for
                desk sergeants twenty-four seven. Pensions
for widows of policemen killed

in line of duty. Insurance for the cars
and personnel.
                    It isn't what thieves steal or terrorists mutilate,
          it's what we do to catch them, stop them, keep
                         them from it. They
generate the law, create police, construct
          our locks and jails, get us treated as
          potential criminals everywhere we go, determine
where we can walk at night. I used to think
          the admen were important, and the CEOs,
free marketeers who set the price of interest.
          Hell, criminals set the price of life.
                    So where are statues to them? Here's one
Poem To the Unknown Criminal, Who
          Makes the World Go Square.

Chimes at Midnight

Dear Walt,
    Well, that was some weekend. Can't see why Janie Bell
    thinks Webb City is just a wide spot in the road,
        unless she means there's never any news
because there's no newspaper there to print it.
    Way things went last weekend though, you all
    will need a RADIO station before too long.
I mean, you'll surely have to get a new preacher, won't you?
and let's hope he won't ever preach a sermon
    like the old one did last Sunday morning there.
    Got up there bashing Satan around
    with a two-by-four practically, but got
so worked up he must have forgot himself
        telling what a sinner he was—I never saw
so many surprised husbands all at one time
    as when he got down to details, and all their wives
    just sitting right there, too dumbfounded to lie.
Didn't take that preacher long to run out
    of cheeks to turn, did it, when they got hold of him—
but I expect the carpenters have fixed
    the doors and things back up by now, and if
        he's really gone to California
    I hope the people out there will do
like the preacher says instead of like he does,
        but out there maybe no one will notice.
    —Listen, have you ever heard any more from that old farmer
that tried to kill us with his thirty-thirty?
        I think we ought to prosecute that guy;
    all we were doing was stealing his watermelons,
and Billy never said till afterwards that we were the third
        bunch that got into his patch that day.
I didn't even know, when I came running across that cornfield
    with the big green melon on my head,
that that was his prize one with the orange meat,
    till the thirty-thirty bullet knocked it to pieces and

the juice ran down my face. Man, it made
my eyes so sticky that when
I was trying to sprint on down the ditch
and ran right over poor little Billy in front of me,
I never stopped to see how he was doing,
but I don't think he even noticed.
Yet why couldn't that farmer just use rock salt in a shotgun?
Him with that rifle, we had to run miles
to get out of range,
along that row of Osage orange trees and out on the prairie,
and even there that big Black Angus bull
would've tromped us into mincemeat if we had not
just got across the pump-rod line in time.
Well, we found out what stinging nettles are—
and I just hope that farmer tries someday to use a few
for toilet paper, the way we did.
There's not much happening, here on this horseless ranch—
come over, though, and we'll find something maybe,
might run some greyhounds out on the prairie
east of Bartlesville—
there's lots of jacks. Might start a coyote even.
P.S. There's a note for Janie Bell enclosed.
Don't open it.
(There wasn't any note for Janey Bell, of course, but maybe she'll
open this one.)

The Secret Verbs

They're hidden right in plain sight.
Take **Unassigned Lands** for instance: what's the verb?
To Unassign.
A powerful verb, in 1889 it grabbed
almost two million acres of Indian lands
where Oklahoma City squats with all
those other towns, wheat farms and ranches
oil wells and politicians.
(Yes, I know how SQUAT infects its many subjects.)
Why call them **Unassigned?**
Well, after the CIVIL War, the Creeks
and Seminoles were forced to concede
this land for settlement by freed slaves.
Quite understandably, no one ever
assigned the land to slaves.
So what that past participle means is this:
We UNASSIGN these lands to Blacks or Indians.
We now ASSIGN them to Americans,
so long as they are WHITE.

That's all the grammar lesson for today,
but for tomorrow, why not look around
at other participles and adjectives
which have deleted agents and unspoken objects
and which are negative?
You see how powerful they are—
and how they hide their power. And how
like redstriped sheets they cover both
the SUBJECT and the OBJECTS of their actions?
Just for instance,
the words DIScover and COVERt,
or DISinform, or UNAmerican,
or UNused land.
How we UNuse our language
is maybe worth a thought, in a

CENTENNIAL year—and every year's
centennial of something, isn't it?

On the Planet of Blue-eyed Cats

(for Stella)

Some moons of Jupiter are
as big as Earth almost;
its golden ones are sulphur, and its
blue-and-white one ice—
Europa, Io, Ganymede, those old
love-victims of descending Zeus remembered in
their heavenly bodies—and now we
are sending Voyagers to be voyeurs
and catch them in the act
of eruption televised
to Pasadena, where the scientists cheer.
Their children will be flying out to Jupiter themselves,
in Solar Clipper ships may sail
on Mylar wings beyond the baths
of all the western stars,
their wind the sunlight and the sun's enormous
gravity to swing and glide against as red-
tailed hawks may ride updrafts for hours
then drop down on their prey;
but these will sail heavy-bellied back not
with bloody rabbits like the red-tailed hawks,
nor tea like clipper ships from China,
but rocks, brain-food for the
scientists, small pieces of the same old stuff,
but histories different from ours,
alterities to probe identities, the jargon goes.
Sliced up with diamond saws,
roasted in X-ray ovens, they will tell
us when their birthday was, just when
they joined the dancing satellites around
the satellites around the sun and through the
other stars; tell us just where we are
and how we came and where we voyage to.
It takes two things to be;
two places make a where;

two planets make a why.
So what are children for? Geoffrey,
Vanessa, Lawrence, would you please
go out to our back yard, and where your mother
has buried Sappho Prettypaws, who was older
than two of you and had a different history, would you set
a piece of the third planet out from our sun? And if
you hold it up first next to
a star, compare it even to Jupiter with all
those moons, it will not sparkle, but
it gives light back, our back yard's on
a blue star in its heaven—
and if
the little green star-people should come down
to check earth out before your children sail
out through their stars, you can
report to them that here a cautious blue-eyed
cat once walked upon and is a part
of earth which they have come to take. Maybe
you can tell by looking at them
how much they follow what you've said to them.
There is so much to understand in even
the simplest human acts,
even the simplest human love, say
of that shy kitten your mother raised,
her wordless judgment of our acts,
her choosing over and over
your mother as beloved,
as trustworthy, when Sappho
was having kittens and she knew
your mother was there for her, and she let
her fondle them and purred, knowing and trusting
this was her friend.
And if those little
green persons understand, even just

a part of what you've said, why then you'll have
a thoughtful friend among the starry powers,
maybe someone for whom
the earth is not a source
of wealth, of slaves, of power, but is
a place where mothers keep alive
what all such voyagers come to find,
wherever wandering matter gives them place
and time and mind to live,
to move, to learn a little of
what beings mean.

A Song That We Still Sing

On the way from Oklahoma up to the Sun Dance
at Crow Dog's Paradise on the Rosebud Sioux Reservation,
they'd stopped a few minutes,
my Ponca cousins from Oklahoma—
they were way out there by some kind
of ruins, on the August prairie,
some kind of fort it may
have been, they stopped
to eat a little, get out and
stretch their legs, the van
had got too little for
the kids and all.
And they were walking
not paying much attention and they heard
the singing and then Casey said,
Listen, that's Ponca singing.
Hear it. Where's it coming from?
They listened, and Mike said,
Sounds like it's over
inside those walls or whatever
they may be, over there.
So they walked
through the dry short grass
towards the raised earth walls
and up on them, and looked
inside that wide compound, and there
was not a soul in sight.

That was a Wolf Song, Mike said.
Yes, a Victory Song, Casey said.

When they told me later, we looked and
decided that it was where the Cheyennes
and some of their allies had chased some troopers
inside a fort and

taunted them—
after Sand Creek it was,
that time the news got out of what
had been done to Black Kettle and
his people there beneath
that big American flag which they'd been given
in token that this peaceful band
was not to be attacked,
and then at dawn the Reverend Colonel
Chivington and his men attacked and massacred
some hundreds who could not escape—
one small boy, running
for refuge, was shot down at a hundred yards,
because, as Chivington had told his troops,
Nits make lice. The women's breasts,
sliced off, were made into
tobacco pouches, as were the scrotums
of men. George Bent, a half-Cheyenne who was there,
who'd been a Confederate soldier and
both wrote and spoke English and Cheyenne,
has told about it in his letters—
he saw White Antelope come out
unarmed from his tepee, pointing up
at Old Glory waving over the village there,
then when the troopers kept on shooting,
he stood unmoved and sang, as they shot him down,
the death-song he'd composed for such a time:

Nothing lives long
except the earth and the mountains.

So I asked Casey and Mike,
what do you think you heard, inside that place?
—*I guess,* Mike said, *up in Nebraska*
there must have been some Poncas

who joined the Cheyennes there and fought
the soldiers till they chased them
into that fort.
Then Casey said,
We recognized that song. It's one
that we still sing.

Starring America

These neon lights are to stars
what Odysseus is to Dwight
Eisenhower—the way you've seen them there
at night, coming down to
LaGuardia over the glittering
inside-out cathedrals of
commerce under the dim
windows of your plane, looking down
past the massive tilting wing with its magically
shifting ailerons, its insect-like
adjustments, creaks and thumps that
keep us flying as we
drop downward cushioned against the screaming
hell of jets
just feet away, sinking into the fume
and grumble of traffic as we princes of
the middle air look at headlights like
souls gliding in Dante's *Paradiso* smoothly along
their destined ways, ruby
tail-lights among bright gold demoglyphs for soup
and motels, twinkling jewels that
Earth must be glad to wear, that make her
seem *fairer than the evening air*
clad in the beauty of a thousand stars—
and surely Marlowe's Helen
or Shakespeare's Cleopatra never
slipped into words more brilliant than
this *multitudinous space incarnadined* to which we now
descend with ordinary lives and dirty
socks, down into
glowing, unreadable words which as we touch
earth gather into signs
of ordinary sleaze: close up, the city's like an

[133]

un-Midased Doppelganger of pond-scum that under
　　　　the microscope bustles with alien beings, just
　　　　　　　　dissolves and pretends
　　　　to be like us ... Bricks, asphalt, glassy hustle,
　　　　　　　　smog-dazzle, horn-blare.
　　　　　But I was going to say,
　　　when literature broke in with all
her fancy words about Cleo and Helen, not just that all these lights
　　　　　　　　are exquisite when seen
　　　　　　　　　　from far enough away, but that
　　　　so much of all this brilliance illuminates
　　　　our fear of violence and greed. I know, that sounds
　　　　eccentric: what I'm driving at is how
　　　　　　　these lights just aren't NEEDED
　　　　to spotlight things: no one would HAVE to see
the highways all that clearly, nor do showcase windows
　　　along Broadway HAVE to be lit at night.
　　　　　　　They do, I understand, shine partly
　　　　　　　　　to MAKE us want
　　　　　　　their jewels, airbrushed sex, their magic
　　　　carpets to the Hesperides glowing in
　　　　　　　　lightfilled windows—
　　　　　　　　　but still,
each light-spell's meant in part to KEEP OUT
the smash and grab of those who can't afford
　　　　Hesperidean fruit, who'd settle
for just one crunch of the Big Apple, worms and all, wanting
　　　　　　the lineaments of gratified desire.
　　　　　　　Looked down on from
　　　a middle heaven, they are beautiful—but then,
　　　　　　　those blue lights set along
　　　　the campus paths, they're RAPE lights, and
they are quite beautiful, aren't they? Messages
　　　of want or violence down there, they all
　　　　　　　look glorious from above.

[134]

NO, NO! JUST TAKE
those motel signs (you say): NOT placed
from fear, but Good Samaritans, to heal the woes of
wayfaring strangers—and what's bought
by crown jewels spilling from Best Western
signs into our midnight windshields is only
hope, is comfort, bright enough
to see from far off shining there.
And that's true too.
And yes,
these signs of fear and
faith are costlier than Cleo's imperial gems and
snakes; the wealth of many continents must
be burned to set their many colors glowing, and they speak
the loveliest art our merchants of desire
have yet invented: one that transforms
a sleazy, murderous Times Square
of smogdom and Gomorrah into
Elysium by night, a brilliant mob
of souls *dwelling*
in possibility,
a fairer house than prose, and just
the place to go and become a star amid
the towered glitter that so many
blacklunged miners, cancerous breasts keep lifting
up toward the stars, high over
that sparkling babble of many tongues below.

2. New York, With Reservations

In the Hotel Empire's coffee shop
        at Sixty-Third and Broadway
    across from Lincoln Center, facing
        the cold bronze back of Dante's statue
in its patch of pigeoned greenery,
    we are waited on hand and foot, Stella and I,
            then red lights part
        the sea of traffic so we can cross
to a promontory flowing with honeyed singers
of Strauss, Stravinsky, Berlioz, where graceful
as a trained dolphin the Hudson River
    leaps from the plaza's fountains, and on
        a day of cold falling rain, a night
of icebound gutters, the seats
            are plush and warm, the stage
    played on by lights that materialize
the Nightingale, danced by Makarova, and
    the Fisherman, danced by Anthony Dowell, delivering
        from death the Chinese Emperor—with singers
in dim orchestral limbo gilding with brilliant sound
    the dancing lilies, until great storms
            of applause conjure through parted
curtains the dancers, singers, orchestra
            conductor ... and now the starburst
    chandeliers relume, descending sparkling as
            the audience rises, and we go,
    Stella and I, into a special room
            for Met supporters, and acting like
                teenagers, have champagne.
—The people in this Belmont Room
    are quieter, more silver-haired;
            like Alistair Cooke they only grace
    a Master Work, so this must be

Our Gracious Study. These waiters who are bringing
                    Champagne, with one Coca-Cola for
the St. Louis friends who hailed us in the lobby,
                    are New York versions of
                    Lord Byron's best valet.
        Elysium indeed: a hotel
                    not expensive, two days and
three nights of music, salmon mousse and hot
        steamed chocolate with whipped cream,
        a friend from Amherst (who survived
with his daughter the plane's crash off Cuba by swimming
        a day and night till they were picked up),
                    and nights in soft beds
with time and privacy and maids to repair, replace
        each morning what is crumpled, soiled,
                    crumb-laden, wet, used up.
        So when we exit, and come under
the green-bronze glare of Dante, we are not
        yet ready to abandon hope, but flying as
gold-carded citizens within the Empire's
        most affluent city we will depart
on shining wings and soaring above its storms return
                    to the Father of Waters and our small
        teacherly tasks: driving Vergilian Rome and
        Dantesque Florence into the heart
                    of this America.

3. On The Reservation

On a cold clear night in March, driving
through the Osage Reservation in Oklahoma towards
                    the old home, I saw
              from the hill's crest down to the east
where once were miles of darkness under the stars
              and moon, where wide
         prairie and woods had held the firefly glow
of distant houses along the rutted
ungraveled roads, there now are blue-white
         mercury lamps, whole constellations quilting
              the soft darkness, at night turned on
                    by automatic switches,
         blacked out by dawn. Beyond the prairie height
more eastward, where light had first spewed up around the new
    radome and barracks of the Cold War's start, now
              misting from the horizon is a smog of light
                    from Bartlesville that dims the stars.
              I think it's the NEW WORLD rising
              like midnight dawn, and it shines
         only for safety: weeknights by eleven,
              everything there is closed except
the lovers' lanes, and those (I hope) are dark. The hum
              of generators laps our citizens
              in light-cocoons. Maybe the darkness
         between real stars is just too heavy, maybe
that makes us drag down heaven, hitch the fossil stars
              of coal and oil and uranium
              to our Volkswagens.
              As for the cost, of course each burning light
                    illumines some poor soul, keeps busy
some poor devil: oil men, service stationers, builders of dams
         and nuclear plants.
                    And if we try to dismount from

our star-striped tiger, we may slide
into his Heart of Darkness.
Ride him to glory, then!
And just consider
how all these things provide
new images for poetry, so needful if
the Epic of America shall be written; and
without an epic, EVERY empire crumples. Even,
perhaps, WITH one.
And yet, wheeling
around the Osage Reservation with my one
surviving uncle of six, I was shaken
by what we saw, leaving Pawhuska: only
a vacant lot, dead neat grass around
the central square of earth where once
wine-red bricks of the old
hospital held us as we seven children fell into
the Dust Bowl and the Great Depression.
Red local bricks, or from
St. Louis, that Grandpa Alex hauled
with mules, Old Beck and Jude, for the builders there.
Dissolved into thin air, an empty space where all our folks
walked down the second-floor corridor to see new baby
brothers and sisters when they appeared, the little
Indian babies next to our mother pale and
darkhaired lying in
that hospital built when Pawhuska was a frantic
boomtown ablaze with oil and honkytonks and
swindlers, plenty of work for men
and mules, plenty of money flowing
through Osage Headright families undigested to
fertilize the farms and double-entry files
of lawyers, bankers, doctors, fattening raucous flocks
of workers hauling its bricks and timbers, all our white
uncles and Grandpa telding up hotels and

jails, and patronizing the latter
more than the former. And building
the hospital, where my Uncle Woody
once lay pillowed trying hard to talk, his tongue
split and his eyes black and swollen, his nose
broken from crashing that jalopy, but still happy
to see his sister Thelma's kids come visit him, then
as now. Yeah, I see
the night-light glowing in his room, his black
and greeny-purple face turn towards us, his sore mouth
crack to a grin as my mother
asked how in the hell it happened,
and his split-tongued lisp telling
how they'd come bucketing round the curve
at sixty miles an hour to see the headlights
on their side of the road and how they had
to hit the ditch. And my mother laughing, glad
no one was killed.
Well,
this lot is vacant and the new hospital's down
in Indian Camp, where the Pawhuska folks can go
and visit now their newly born, stove up or sick. Here now is
only a wintry lawn, the bed of scarlet cannas
gone that had always bloomed when
we visited. Things change. And so the pipelines
fan out grandly with natural gas and oil from here to
New York City. Beneath those mercury lamps, twinkling
out there in the Osage Hills, a family sleeps within
its pool of light, never on
the porch in summertime telling stories but
inside before the glowing screen that tells
of countries we are saving or creating over
one ocean or another, all
by courtesy of Babylon on the Hudson.
What was it like, I wonder, when

we bought this Reservation back from
        the Cherokees, persuaded that the whites would never
        covet these scrub-oak hills and rocky prairies, only
            a hundred and twenty years ago?
                The stories
            were what we made, the stars we cast
ourselves into when we were named. Small wonder all
                those city kids kept running
            away to live with Indians, making up
new lives instead of taking those they were told by Bostonians and
        New Yorkers. How could they,
    fleeing into our darkness, know it was death
            they'd bring the elders in our lodges watching with
                half-shut eyes how close the savage
            Empire was upon us with its sabred troopers ringing
                our Reservation, barbarians on
the borders driving buggies over the line to picnic, choosing
            the homesites for that day when earth
                would be allotted, measured, sold.
                    So the outlaws flocked
among us, brought us News ... Whiskey ... Statehood And
            Watermelons, made us the white
            Forty-sixth Star blowing in
        the wind. Join and/or die. So now
        we CAN fly easily across
    this continent where less and less
is dark and "empty." Maybe just to marinate in
the Dantesque brilliance of New York's City's better
than frying in the friendly holocaust reserved
            for our Lost Tribes. And so our
                Empire draws us all together, all
    our stories turn to HIStory, all the old
Republic's cities into one great city, waiting for that Vergil from
                the distant provinces who'll lead
            Columbia's heroes up to the Stars,

past Death itself they say.
                    But you,
            they say, *pagan forerunners,*
                    you must go down again
into your Limbo: having (they say) *served us in our need,,*
                    your proper role is now to
            vanish: *to be forever deaf*
    to all salvation's song, and without all hope to hear.
                    Someone, you know, must pay
                    for all the glittering
enlightenment we bring up from the dark below
            this earth you had not really used.

Over There

Advice from Euterpe

They hire you for the silk to line their budgets,
        they give you immortal tenure
           among their well-thumbed leaves
                until you spin—
     but you must never come out
          of that cocoon: your life's the single thread
             spun for their satiny profit.
So, if they should discover
        that you're no spinner and have been chewing
           apart on your *Asclepias* leaves,
                    you'd better split that instant,
   shake out your wings on the wind and rise
          like a Monarch to the pungence waiting
               in mountain meadows where
       snow-water leaps—
           on wings too bright and bitter
           for the hookbilled shrike to swallow.

Jetliner from Angel City

Earthborn of white
Titanium sand in Magnesium shell from
the foamy sea, I stretch forth from
their silver ark long wings hung
with four hells driving heavenward my
Cave of Vulcan where frozen
chicken boogies high with microwaves over
a shimmer of crimson cloud for a gym-floor, high
over the Mother Of Snowy Wrinkles with all
her dark pines, bears, mountain lions, the
Grand Canyon's sliding silence,
among faint stars around full moon, high
over a neon-jeweled octopus raping the seashore as
I cocoon in home and history strangers hurtling
to China, to Peru, to Inner Space where the
moon is white gold among snowbank clouds over
rivers, oceans, volcanoes,
time-warps ahead and behind us, looking down on
Greenland's icy mountains, pyramids
of San Francisco, Chicago, Cairo, Chichén Itzá,
step in from Siberian winter,
walk out to Samoan summer—
Ah folks, this is your Captain speaking.
Notice that flight of swans
or whooping cranes passing below,
and over there a spectacular
thundercloud's charcoal and salmon castle
gold-lit by swarms of lightning bugs
laid on especially for our flight—
next week we race this century's last
total eclipse's shadow into night, today we're just
your silver dove returning to the earth.

Where the Muses Haunt

Yet not the more
Cease I to wander where the Muses haunt,
Clear spring, or shady grove, or sunny hill . . .

Neither the honey nor the honeybee . . .

Atop the Opéra Garnier in Paris there's
an apiary, lots of beehives where
the bees make honey from the flowers
of all the parks and gardens in that City of Light—
the keeper of those bees has said the honey's finer
than from his hives in the countryside
because Paris has so many exotic
flowers where the bees can gather
nectar and pollen, sweet as though from
Manet and Renoir paintings of *la vie en rose*, fragrance of
blossoms in the Jardins de Luxembourg, the Tuileries,
from windowbox and lindenbaum,
orangeries, and why not roses around the tombs
of Baudelaire, Ronsard, and Mallarmé—or, for all
that music hived in l'Opéra Garnier,
the graves of Massenet and Gounod?

And high up on Mount Ida there were small bees
on those dry herbal thorns, humming
and gathering where goldfinches flitted,
when we were looking (like Saturn) for
the Dictæan Caves where Zeus was born
and the Curetes howled to drown his wawling—
and down in Minoan vales new cicadas
were singing over the great ruined palaces
of Knossos, and those of Phaistos,
while tourists wandered quietly under pines
stepping on baked hard earth with its holes
where those Muses' Daughters

after their seventeen dark years had come up
to sing in the pines over the ragged rooms
of the Blue Dolphins and the Dancing Ladies—
one of whom came up
to take our orders as the waitress
in our seaside hotel that night, her profile and
her dark hair's curls and ruby smile
exactly theirs, at seventeen.

And in Jerusalem, that herbal smell—and the small
white-rumped bees were humming around the Tombs
of the Patriarchs—later
on Cyprus by the broken columns
of Apollo's temple butterflies were floating, nymphs
and satyrs, naturally—

and then we were whisked
zigzagging in a Mercedes taxi up and up
on the Isle of Patmos to the monastery with St. John's
pillow of stone and its gold-and-incense relics of
his Revelation—though what got to me
was a cobalt bay with white cruise ships waiting beside
the town's cafes and tourist shops under
a sky of luminous blue with two peregrine
falcons hovering, quick wingbeats ready
to tower and stoop like meteors into the flight
of white doves veering panicky over orange roofs—but
the falcons circled and winged away,
the doves spiraled out and back over
the harbor's blue—and while we waited
for a taxi to take us down again the bees
went on with their gathering from the pale blue
rosemary and from thyme.

The Swan's Song
(from the "Exeter Book")

Garbed in silence   I go on earth,
dwell among men   or move on the waters.
Yet far over halls   of heroes in time
my robes and the high   air may raise
and bear me up   in heaven's power
over all nations.   My ornaments then
are singing glories,   and I go in song
bright as a star,   unstaying above
the world's wide waters,   as a wayfaring soul.

Pilotless Angel: Christmas, 2004

From soot I rise: bright red my eye,
Night-black my body: bat-wings rigid,
Sharp gold-wired brain   aware and circling,
I beam the phantom   faces up
Of families who sit   sipping sweet coffee,
Set them in a cannon's   unseen cross-hairs,
Small moving creatures   marked for death.

Letter to Friends on the Isle of Skye

Dear Frankie, Maud, and Joe,
        I'm sitting here, sunk
in sloth and St. Louis, and even though
        last night when I was walking
                a yellow blinking light
spread gold upon the rain-glazed street
        ahead of me and behind,
its only word was *Caution!* so I keep thinking how
                on the Isle of Skye the golden
        eagles came down, where Joe
                and I were standing on
the waterfall's edge to see the stream
slip glinting down its green vale that quivered like
        a wineglass half-filled with purple
ocean, and I was watching
        the brown quick wren below us bobbing
                into crevices among   ·
great mossy boulders of
        the pyramid island beneath
                the falls, popping out
through heather-fringe and sending
        her silver needle-trill
                through swash and champagne thunder,
then pouncing neatly
        on pillbugs in the dust and
                darkness of their crevice,
and coming out swallowing, swallowing with
        her wings akimbo and her
                eyebead cocked
        towards us watching above—and
leaning over the fall-edge, looking down
        on the wren's darting
        business, my senses
        gurgling with plastic silver
        music, a sudden flick

of my eye ripped one
    trilling free from bird-beak and pinned it down by
my boot, to a rock-jut warbling
    its wave-spray flute in the throat
of the waterfall's tuba and waked
      in my ears the voices
        of birds before sunrise streaming
          here from stones, from ripples,
    and putting my head
up under a granite slab as into
    a seashell's concert heard
the ringing of mockingbird changes on
oboes—mosquitoes—coloraturas over
    the cataract's bass viol grumbling
upstream—and turning to see that music
    instead saw hanging
    ten feet over water
    great dark brown bird
    his yellow eye watching
us, and the wren, and the twinkling sea—and
    he rose as I turned,
      he steered with his
      spread tail as heavy as
        a Viking ship turning
        in the aircurrents over
        the stream, he swung and
sailed downwind to leftward,
    as my voice came back and I said
    "Turn around, Joe—binoculars!"
and you remember Joe how you turned
    and it scared the piss out of you so
      you nearly fell over seeing
that great glaring head down
    and his grappling talons lowered as
he swung into the wind and rose

again up the cliffside, floated
            out over the stream
            crossing in silence
            above its flashing noise,
                        and finding an updraft rose higher,
                            floating up shelf by shelf
to the clifftop,
                and over, being joined in
                            the distance by
                    two others soaring high
                against white clouds
                            and quartering off
            to hunt down the steep sides
of Lorigill where red grouse
            and hares would be hiding in bracken—but
                before they had quite vanished,
plunging out from the rock-juts beneath
                their great easy circles came
        two ravens, fleeing
voiceless and panicked, flapping across
with black undulations till nearing
            the other clifftops they swung smoothly apart
                like boys on rollerskates with a flourish
                        to land among broken rocks,
            then looked back and croaked
                defiance of great gold bullies,
strutting their elegant blackness and laughter
            as though just returned from taking,
                    back in that wilderness of rocks,
                        to the prophet Elijah
                        his daily bread.

Postcolonial Hyperbaggage

If only Vuitton would make a suitcase
with modem and hypertext—or at least windows
to let us put new folders in, where
jackets won't wrinkle and all
the smelly socks can be hung with care in
the hyperspace herb-drawer—and with
still cooler files whose chocolate
truffles would never melt
into a cashmere sweater. We need these
neat reversible black holes for crossing Borders,
things we could pack and close
at a single touch and never pop a seam
or rip a zipper. They'd make the Eurodollar
            zoom up in value—
and hey, just think,
Stealth Bombers could be replaced
        by diplomatic pouches full
of virtual assassins,
used terrorists could be dumped
        out of the Trash Can, leaving
            a Virtuous Reality.
All Indian Reservations could be *desaparecidos*
        into Death Valley, yet accessible through
                their golden icon, the Sacajawea Dollar.
        Such a Pandora's Apple, I think,
                even the seediest Satan could have sold
        to the smartest Adam and Eve, just by saying
                one taste of this, my dears,
                        and you're back in Eden.

Columbus Looks Out Far, In Deep

(For Robert Frost, who said America is hard to see.)

What I don't see, after five hundred years,
is what the coral sees,
or abalone, how the tubeworms send
their wavering scarlet, pale lavender petals out
into the surge and quiver,
the beating drift of food raining down into
their waiting moving tendrils and blind
mouths, turquoise and crimson
fish lifting and turning in Pollock symphonies
of play and feeding—
what I don't know
is whether they can see their genes,
know what they'd like to be, MizDoss
the molecules and become just that—
I don't see whether
they vote, excite the hydra-headed mob
to flail its tendrils, whether all
the schools of fish in sync
and Zeitgeist sense
the coming crisis from an ozone hole
or asteroid's catastrophe—

what media they may use to publicize
the whitening of coral skeletons along
a thousand miles of reef,
the driftnets strangling dolphins,
great ghostly sharks wavering past impoisoned,
the seals with cancerous growths,
translucent jellyfish beached and stinking—
they have no way of knowing, surely,
that clumsy breathing creatures dipping
delighted toes into the shallow sandy blue,
so helpless, innocent and silly,
are killing them. Though maybe,
like wildebeest watching lions,

they know, they know,
but that's the way it is, and they may trust
their speed, or think that day by day
they've seen these creatures come and go,
and not been chosen for the slaughter.

—Or could it be they *know*
what's waiting for us killers—
plutonium tank-shells, asteroids,
death's claws beneath the unlocked gate of
midnight, or wading out of
tomorrow like Godzilla's child?
Maybe they see through worm-holes
into the future,
maybe they have a time-line open
along their own dimension,
foresee the fading out of human
awareness, going to sleep
and waking without bodies there,
adrift and shoreless,
not knowing where the past has gone,
drifting and drifting in a fragile film
of moisture on a drifting globe, merely
one drop of water in an ocean, salty as tears
and blood, an acid trip
without an end, the only hope
to let go and not understand,
not see, not hear, not know,
not try to be.

But Still in Israel's Paths They Shine

Six hundred dark feet the cliffs
　　from the crash of Atlantic swells
　　　　beetle up over their surf
　　and its patches of seaweed tangling
　　　　the waves's drive shoreward
pulsed by the miles-off gray of storms
　　into this sunlit scene, to
　　　　us seated on green headland
　　with slow-grazing sheep dotted whitely along
gentle slopes to the lighthouse
　　looking across that wave-thrash at blurred
　　　　rock-bands and strata holding each
a million years of sleet and blossoms crushed
　　to a band of brown, to
　　　　us thinking how
　　down on that shingle walking
we saw this morning the million
pebbles brought down from the cliffs's monochrome to lie
all streaked and dappled, spotted and milky and veined,
　　　　not one like another but all
　　　　rounded and smoothly
　　rubbing together in wetness; to us
　　　　remembering how
down in the tidal pool's depths by the boulders
　　a powder-blue jellyfish was pulsing
upward and downward in that bluegreen clearness,
　　　　as fragile as joy in time,
　　yet riding the Atlantic's power; to us
climbing down at noontime all
　　　　the way to the stream's mouth where
　　its last waterfall pours whitely down
　　　　to the cove and its peppersalt beach;
　　to us seeing in noon-light how the tiny
　　　　　　crab-spiders sidle upon
　　　　sand-brilliants and

                    its grains rough-shaped on palms
    as the cliffs where white seabirds soar and
                    dive,
        grains crowding like white
                    faces in terminal lobbies eroded
                    by grief and joy, pouring
        from the hand like pieces
of broken planets tumbling
                    and flashing
        in space, saying:
                    the revolution we work for
                    is revelation and the eyes to see
        these shining things and how
                    they change, and pass,
                    and are the same.

Songs of the Wine-throated Hummingbird
(with thanks to Alexander Skutch's "The Life of the Hummingbird")

Down in the sapphire ocean
            the Humpback whales are singing,
maybe about the wonders there,
        how light changes as they descend so that
        their silver day becomes
                a sable night,
or about those whippersnapper bottlenoses blowing
    great shimmering bubbles then piercing like
            spears the silver-quivering
bag of a rising bubble—even as high within
        its green radiance of Guatemalan forest
                a wine-throated
        hummingbird's "sweetly varied outpouring
            continues for the better part
        of a minute"
                —ah, if only
            the whales and dolphins swam
    in *that* green light, and heard
those tiny singers in their sea of leaves,
        such arias they'd interchange,
La Ci Darem La Mano from a great dark whale,
Un Bel Di from high in the frangipani—and then,
                imagine the duets,
        O Terra Addio at the top
    of a dolphin's range, in the center of
            a rubythroat's fioritura—
                    of course
            they sing together only
in human words, never I guess in any
            but English ones in fact—
    in these, if anywhere. Can you hear,
            dear reader, how
they sing, you above all who from Africa
    brought banjoes and picked up saxophones
        then sang the blues all out

of slaveship holds to Harlem, you from every
ocean and continent who understand the songs
of police and ambulance sirens, who record the stars
or white noise from the first Big Bang, is it beyond
our imagining how the humpback and
the hummingbird might come out
through parted curtains at the Met for a last
encore. What are sounds,
and what are songs, that we can make them,
that we have ears to hear,
that on these tiny waves
of air, of water, even of magnetism, we have made
the smaller ripples that we call Meaning
when sounds are words—or which, rising
like Aphrodite from the foam
of dance and song and love, come through as Music. Deep
in the blue Antarctic seas, high
in the green Guatemalan jungle, here
in these cracked English words,
can you hear them sing,
the hummingbirds, the humpback whales,
a neutron star, a human soul?